THE TOP 100 DIET SECRETS

THE TOP 100 DIET SECRETS

ANNA SELBY

DUNCAN BAIRD PUBLISHERS

LONDON

The Top 100 Diet Secrets
Anna Selby

First published in the United Kingdom and Ireland in 2008 by
Duncan Baird Publishers Ltd
Sixth Floor
Castle House
75–76 Wells Street
London W1T 3QH

Conceived, created and designed by
Duncan Baird Publishers

This edition published 2008 for Index Books Ltd

Managing Editor: Grace Cheetham
Editor: Zoë Stone
Managing Designer: Suzanne Tuhrim
Designer: Gail Jones
Commissioned photography: Simon Smith and Toby Scott

British Library Cataloguing-in-Publication Data:
A CIP record for this book is available from the British Library

ISBN: 978-1-84483-363-4

10 9 8 7 6 5 4

Typeset in Helvetica Condensed
Colour reproduction by Colourscan, Singapore
Printed in China by Imago

Publisher's Note: The information in this book is intended as a healthy guide to dieting and is not meant as a substitute for professional medical advice and treatment. The foods and recipes contained in this book are intended for adults. If you are pregnant or breastfeeding or have any special dietary requirements or medical conditions, it is advisable to consult a medical professional before following any of the information or recipes contained in this book. The publishers and the author cannot accept responsibility for any errors or omissions, inadvertent or not, that may be found in the recipes or text, nor for any problems that may occur as a result of preparing one of the recipes or following the diet advice contained in this work. All recipes serve four unless specified otherwise.

CONTENTS

INTRODUCTION 6

FRUITS 14
Watermelon, Pineapple, Kiwi
fruit, Grape, Peach, Fig, Apple,
Apricot, Melon, Pear, Mango,
Banana, Papaya, Prune, Cherry,
Berries, Orange, Lemon, Lime,
Grapefruit

VEGETABLES 36
Sweet potato, Carrot, Onion,
Potato, Garlic, Leek, Celeriac,
Radish, Tomato, Red pepper,
Avocado, Beetroot, Cucumber,
Courgette, Mushroom, Broccoli,
Globe artichoke, Asparagus,
Chicory, Spinach, Watercress,
Cabbage, Kale, Aubergine,
Lettuce, Nettle, Sorrel, Celery,
Fennel, Seaweed

GRAINS AND PULSES 70
Bulgur wheat, Rye, Oats,
Wild rice, Brown rice, Psyllium,
Quinoa, Barley, Wholewheat
pasta, Lentil, Chickpea, Soya,
Sprouted seeds, Alfalfa

NUTS AND SEEDS 86
Nuts, Pine nuts, Seeds

PROTEIN 90
Salmon, Mackerel, Sardine,
Cod, Tuna, Oyster, Prawn,
Chicken, Turkey, Liver,
Partridge, Venison, Duck,
Egg, Tofu

DAIRY 107
Low-fat cheese, Ricotta cheese,
Fromage frais, Bio yogurt,
Low-fat milk

DRINKS 113
Green tea, Herbal tea, Water,
Juices, Smoothies

**OILS, HERBS, SPICES AND
FLAVOURINGS** 119
Olives and olive oil, Honey,
Carob, Vegetable bouillon,
Spices, Chilli, Herbs, Ginger

INDEX 128

KEY TO DIET SECRETS

- low-fat
- low carb
- low GI
- low GL
- low calorie
- low kilojoule
- detoxifying
- dairy-free
- gluten-free
- wheat-free

Introduction

Diet secret number 1 – "diets" don't work. The ever-rising statistics on the numbers of overweight people are testament to this. Any diet which is based on quick-fix ideas might seem to work at first but it is usually impossible to sustain. And when you give up the regime, of course, all the weight you lost comes piling back on.

Shockingly, many of these diets can actually be bad for you, too, limiting the range of foods and so the range of nutrients that you eat. In the case of high-protein and low-carb diets, for example, this can lead to a lack of necessary vitamins, constipation and even bone deterioration. With diets that focus on one food or group of foods (remember the cabbage soup diet?) you will probably find that, although you may well experience dramatic weight loss, you will regain the weight when you inevitably return to your normal diet. Often the reason these diets seem to work at first is that you lose fluid rather than fat. Disappointment follows, as does yo-yo dieting, in the effort to keep the pounds off. Finally the body – faced with the threat of starvation – clings to the food it receives and flatly refuses to lose any more weight.

However, don't despair. There are proven ways to lose weight successfully, and I will show you them. The first thing to do is to choose the right foods and cook them properly. This is the first secret of successful weight loss. On the following pages I offer more secrets: the main food groups that you need to be both slim and healthy, together with information on what really works, including explanations on GI and GL, low-carb and low-fat diets and detox foods, and then 100 of these foods and how to prepare them. Some of the foods are well known to dieters, others less so. But together they form the basis of a healthy diet that can be sustained over time to ensure you lose those unwanted pounds – and keep them off.

FOOD GROUPS FOR WEIGHT LOSS
FRUITS
Fruits make delicious, healthy, low-calorie and low-fat snacks or desserts and are one of the most important parts of our diet. In many recent diet fads – such as Atkins – they play a very limited role or are excluded altogether because of their natural sugar content. In fact, without fruit you miss out on a range of vital nutrients and their powerful cleansing action on the system, particularly the digestive tract, that is crucial to the dieter.

A healthy digestive system is a key factor in succeeding at weight loss. Improving your digestion increases your ability to absorb essential nutrients from foods, which regulate all bodily processes. Poor digestive health can leave your body nutritionally depleted and unable to regulate essential functions efficiently, which can lead to water retention and weight gain as well as health problems.

Fruits are packed with fibre, which stimulates the digestive system, encouraging peristalsis (the muscular contractions of the bowel) and preventing constipation. This, in turn, helps avoid bloating and water retention.

Owing to their natural sugar content, some fruits will have a high GI – though they will generally have a low GL (see page 12). Fruits also contain lots of water and this helps to rehydrate the body and prevent the digestive system from becoming sluggish, thus aiding metabolism and fat-burning. The benefits of including fruit in your diet go beyond helping you stay slim. People who eat lots of fruit have healthy skin and hair and a radiant glow. Make sure you eat plenty of fruit every day as part of your diet plan.

VEGETABLES
The importance of vegetables for the dieter cannot be overstated. Low in calories and fat, they are highly nutritious, containing a whole range of vitamins and minerals that will keep you healthy while you are trying to lose weight. At the same time, they introduce

healthy fibre to the diet, ensuring the digestive system is working properly, clearing away toxins and keeping the body hydrated, yet banishing water retention. And they have fabulous skin-boosting properties, too.

The best way to eat vegetables is fresh and raw. Raw food makes the body work harder in digestive terms and by using more energy it has less fat to store. Most vegetables can also be juiced if you have a juicer (see page 13) and, though you miss out on some of the fibre, juicing is a great way of consuming vitamins and minerals. Never leave vegetables to soak in water before cooking. Instead, peel and chop them immediately before you need them. Any kind of cooking destroys some of the nutrients in vegetables, so cook them lightly to retain as much goodness as possible. Steaming is the quickest and best way to cook green, leafy vegetables, with boiling second best, but keep the lid on and use only a little water (don't throw the water away at the end – it makes an excellent basis for stock). Baking is another healthy option (though it raises the GL of foods), but use oil sparingly. Don't fry vegetables (except onions and garlic) and avoid microwaving as the jury is still out on whether this will destroy certain nutrients. Dieters should eat a wide range of vegetables per day. If you think of juices, soups, salads and snacks such as crudités, you will see it's actually very easy to achieve.

GRAINS AND PULSES

Grains and pulses do have a high carb element and so do carry a calorie load. It is a mistake, though, to think we don't need carbs – they are a vital part of healthy eating, but we do, however, need to ensure we are getting the right carbs (see page 12; and page 13 for grain intolerances).

There is a lot of confusion about grains and cereals in our diets. They are banned from many low-carb diets, yet other regimes insist on plenty of fibre, notably in the form of bran. The truth is that fibre is essential in the diet but in the form of bran or bran flakes it is often far too harsh for the digestive system, preventing the absorption of other nutrients and causing sensitivity in the gut. The best dietary fibre is found in fruit and vegetables – leave the bran on the supermarket shelf.

Wholegrains (such as brown or wild rice, bulgur wheat and barley) and pulses (such as chickpeas, soya beans and lentils) are a fantastic low-fat source of fibre, promoting a healthy digestive tract and helping to protect the lining of the colon. They also boost energy and regulate blood-fat levels.

NUTS AND SEEDS

Most nuts and seeds are rich in healthy fats and are good protein sources, but use in moderation as they are often high in calories.

PROTEIN

We need protein for cellular growth and repair and it is an essential part of our diet – but a relatively small one. Protein is found in a wide range of foods including fish, meat, poultry, game, dairy products, eggs, beans and lentils, nuts, seeds and tofu. Some of these foods are high in fat or have heavy cholesterol loads, but all can be eaten in moderation, if properly prepared.

Meat, poultry and game

When cooking animal protein, it is important to trim all the fat (and skin in the case of poultry) and cook them in a way that reduces the fat further rather than adding to it. There are plenty of cooking tips under the individual entries in the book. Always start with the raw ingredient rather than buying processed meals that contain lots of undesirable additives – usually including salt and sugar. Avoid any "coated" meat or poultry, such as those in breadcrumbs or self-basting products, and go for organic or free-range.

Fish and seafood

These are generally lower in fat than animal proteins. However, always buy as fresh as possible and avoid any coated fish. Tinned fish is also good for dieters (though sometimes not so beneficial nutritionally), but check that it has not been canned with oil or undesirable additives.

Other proteins

Protein is available from a wide range of non-meat sources. Eggs are a good source of protein but they are high in cholesterol, so limit yourself to one or two a week. Tofu and other soya products are excellent vegetarian sources of protein, as are many beans.

DAIRY

Always buy low-fat when it comes to milk, cheese and other dairy produce, as, although they are good sources of protein and calcium, they are high in saturated fat.

DRINKS AND FLAVOURINGS

Drinks and flavourings can, perhaps more than any of the other food categories, make or break your weight-loss plan. This is because they often contain hidden calories, sugar and unhealthy additives. If you drink lots of tea, coffee and cola, you are taking in caffeine which not only robs the body of precious minerals such as magnesium, but also blocks your ability to absorb vitamins. Check out the drinks section of this book for plenty of drinks you can choose that won't pile on the calories, but will rehydrate your body, helping it to function better and particularly promoting digestive health.

Flavourings are put in virtually all foods that are not basic raw ingredients. Even such comparatively simple and healthy options as a loaf of bread or a tin of baked beans contain both salt and sugar. While the reason for avoiding sugar is obvious to anyone who wants to lose weight, salt can also be a problem. Apart from the fact that too much salt in the diet is linked to increased risk of high blood pressure, stroke and heart disease, it also contributes to water retention and, in turn, bloating. You can wean yourself off salt and sugar cravings – try reducing the amount you use on your plate or in your cooking a fraction at a time and your taste buds will adjust surprisingly quickly. The flavourings section of this book offers alternatives for salt and sugar as well as a wide range of diet-friendly flavourings that taste delicious and will contribute to your weight loss and keep you healthy, too.

WHAT REALLY WORKS

Now let's look at ways of incorporating foods from these food groups in your eating plan. The book covers seven tried and tested approaches to weight loss: low-fat, low carb, low GI and low GL, low calorie and low kilojoule, and detox. For each of the 100 diet foods in the book a set of symbols will tell you at a glance which dieting methods apply to which food. There is a key on the contents page. Many of the foods feature all seven

TOP TEN TIPS FOR WEIGHT LOSS

- Avoid the shelves of processed foods and ready meals in the supermarket. These foods are full of unwanted fats and sugars. Instead, buy simple, fresh, raw ingredients.
- Drink 8 glasses of water a day (you can substitute herbal teas for some of these) to overcome a sluggish digestive system and toxic build-up.
- Control your portions of all foods except vegetables – you can heap those on your plate.
- If you feel hungry between meals, reach for a healthy snack rather than a bar of chocolate or a biscuit. Choose a banana or other fruit, a couple of oatcakes with hummus, some vegetable crudités with cottage cheese or a low-fat bio yogurt.
- Invest in a pedometer and count your steps – try to take 10,000 steps every day.
- Always focus on your food – eat slowly and don't eat while watching TV or walking around.
- Keep your diet varied so you don't lose interest.
- If you suffer from bloating you may have a food intolerance. Try cutting out the most likely suspects and reintroduce them gradually to find the culprit – the most common are wheat, dairy, citrus fruits and eggs.
- Take up skin brushing – it stimulates the circulation of the blood as well as the lymphatic system and breaks down fatty deposits.
- Keep a food and weight loss diary to spur you on and help you identify any problems.

symbols, meaning they are perfect diet foods! The key also shows you which foods are free from wheat, gluten or dairy.

LOW-FAT

We do need to include fat in our diet, but only in small amounts and only the right kinds. There are two basic types of fat – saturated and unsaturated. Saturated fat is mostly found in animal products, such as meat, butter, cream and cheese, but is also often hidden in processed foods (which may also contain trans fats). Saturated fats are not just empty calories but they are harmful, too, linked to increased "bad" LDL blood cholesterol and heart disease. Whereas unsaturated fats are healthy, essential fats, which are vital to our health and may actually lower LDL cholesterol. They are found in vegetable oils, oily fish, olive oils, nuts and avocados. However, all fats should be limited if you want to lose weight.

LOW CARB

Carbs are a basic fuel for energy but nowadays too many of the carbs in our diet come from sugars – in foods such as chocolate bars or fizzy drinks – that rush into our system, give us a brief high and leave us feeling depleted, hungry or even depressed. They also tend to contain lots of calories but with hardly any nutrients – making us gain weight without any nutritional benefit! But slow-release or "complex" carbs, such as rice oats and barley, are ideal for dieters because, although they also often have a high GI, they release a slow-burning energy that keeps hunger pangs at bay and doesn't cause your blood sugar levels to rocket and plummet. As an added bonus, many also release a fat-burning hormone called glucagon. Complex carbs also contain fibre, which is essential to good digestion.

LOW GI AND GL

GI stands for Glycaemic Index. This is a scale that scores the speed with which the carbs of specific foods are digested. In foods with a high GI, this process happens quickly, causing a surge of glucose (the product of digestion) in the bloodstream, which in turn causes the body to release insulin, converting the glucose into fat and storing it in your fat cells. The result is a drop in your blood sugar which triggers a craving for more high-GI foods. This becomes a rollercoaster of fat storing and cravings.

In foods with a low GI, the carbs are broken down slowly, giving a gradual release of glucose, preventing blood sugar highs and lows. They also make you feel fuller for longer, so you will be less likely to binge.

GL stands for Glycaemic Loading. It developed from GI and looks not only at how fast the glucose hits the bloodstream but also at the proportion of carbs contained in the food. For instance, a food may have a high GI rating because its sugar releases quickly but only a small proportion of the food is sugar and so its effect is lower than its GI rating would have you believe. This is particularly the case with many fruits.

LOW CALORIES AND KILOJOULES

A calorie is a unit of energy: the body converts calories contained in foods into energy. One calorie is equal to 4.184 joules.

If a food is low in calories, it will also be low in kilojoules. Low-calorie diets were once the only show in town but many people found them hard to follow because of all the weighing and calculating that they involved. Now calories are seen as a good general guideline to losing weight, but in conjunction with other methods. However, be aware that many low-calorie foods contain other unhealthy ingredients – this applies particularly to many convenience foods.

DETOX FOODS

Certain foods have a deeply cleansing effect on particular organs in the body – especially the liver, the kidneys and the digestive tract that between them do all the hard work when it comes to processing food. When these organs are working at their best, the digestion of food and the way your body uses the nutrients in food will improve. This will not only show on the scales, but you will also see a difference in your skin, hair, eyes and sense of well-being. Most fruits and vegetables are powerful detoxifiers, containing potent antioxidants that work together to encourage good health while you lose weight. A one-day detox on just fruit and fruit juices is a great way to kick-start your weight-loss plan.

For this you will need to buy a juicer: food processors or blenders won't work unless they have a special attachment, but juicers are readily available and inexpensive. Juicing is a great way of getting vitamins, minerals and enzymes and it's a lot easier to drink a glass of carrot juice than it is to munch your way through a pound of carrots!

INTOLERANCES

Some foods – in particular wheat, gluten and dairy – are linked to intolerance. Symptoms can include weight gain, bloating and water retention – the last things the dieter needs. If you think you might have a wheat intolerance, try cutting all wheat and wheat products out of your diet for a week or two and see if you notice a difference. If you think you might have an intolerance to gluten, do the same with foods containing gluten (all wheat and wheat products, plus barley, rye and oats). Then do the same with dairy (milk, butter, cheese and lactose products). There are lots of wheat-/gluten-/dairy-free foods to choose from in the book. Just look for the symbols.

watermelon

NUTRIENTS

Vitamins B5, C, beta-carotene, folic acid; calcium, magnesium, phosphorus, potassium

The vitamin C and beta-carotene in watermelon help protect skin against premature ageing.

As its name suggests, watermelon contains plenty of water – it makes up 92 percent of the fruit – so it is rehydrating as well as delicious.

Watermelon has a high GI (72) but a low GL (10), owing to its high water content. Low in calories, low in sodium and virtually fat-free, watermelon is also loaded with nutrients, particularly vitamin C, making it a superbly healthy diet food. The seeds contain essential fatty acids and protein, so if you juice watermelon, be sure to leave the seeds in.

TROPICAL COCKTAIL

400g/14oz watermelon
400g/14oz pineapple

Remove the hard skin of the watermelon and pineapple and reserve the watermelon seeds. Chop the flesh into chunks and mix together in the juicer. Drink it straight or turn it into a fizzy drink by adding sparkling water.

pineapple

This delicious, sweet, fragrant fruit improves the digestion of protein and cleanses the intestines.

Pineapples contain the enzyme bromelian which aids the digestion of protein in a similar way to the enzyme papain, found in papayas. This fruit cleanses and stimulates the digestive system and also helps to lower cholesterol. It makes a great fresh juice, either on its own or juiced with other fruits, such as apples and bananas – quite different from the pineapple juice you get in a carton.

NUTRIENTS
Vitamin C, beta-carotene, folic acid; calcium, phosphorus, potassium; bromelian

EXOTIC PINEAPPLE SALAD

1 large pineapple
1 mango
1 papaya
handful of raspberries

Slice the pineapple in half and take out the flesh, leaving the shell intact. Chop the pineapple, mango and papaya into chunks and mix with the raspberries. Place in the pineapple shells and serve.

003

◉ ◉ ◉ ◉ ◉ ◉ ◉ ◉ ◉ ◉ ◉

kiwi fruit

NUTRIENTS

Vitamin C, beta-carotene; calcium, iron, magnesium, phosphorus, potassium; bioflavonoids; fibre

KIWI AND REDCURRANT YOGURT

4 kiwi fruits
225g/8oz redcurrants, topped and tailed
2 tsp honey
400g/14oz low-fat bio yogurt

Peel the kiwi fruits, then chop the flesh and mix with the redcurrants, honey and yogurt. Serve in glass bowls.

Kiwi fruits are fantastic for beating water retention.

The fibre in kiwi fruits makes them very effective intestinal cleansers, and they improve the digestive system as well as the immune system. They remove excess sodium from the body which helps to stabilize the water levels in the cells and reduce blood pressure.

Just two kiwi fruits provide twice as much vitamin C as an orange.

grape

Extremely cleansing and sweet, grapes make an ideal alternative for those who crave sugar.

Full of powerful antioxidants, grapes are very effective detoxifiers for the liver, kidneys and digestive system and have a gentle laxative effect. They are high in natural sugars, so have a high GI, but are still a good food for dieters – a small bunch (12 or 15 grapes) makes a delicious dessert or snack.

A grape-only day is a good, quick detox – but drink lots of water, at least eight large glasses.

NUTRIENTS
Vitamins B1, B2, B3, C; calcium, copper, iron, magnesium, phosphorus, potassium, zinc; flavonoids

GRAPE AND PLUM JUICE

1 large bunch red grapes, destalked
7 or 8 plums, washed and stoned

Juice the fruit in a juicer. Stir and drink immediately.

005

peach

NUTRIENTS

Vitamins B3, C, beta-carotene, folic acid; calcium, iron, magnesium, phosphorus, potassium, zinc; flavonoids

Ideal fruit for detoxification, peaches cleanse the digestive system, the kidneys and the bladder.

Peaches (and nectarines) are deliciously sweet fruits with a deep cleansing effect. They are slightly diuretic and laxative, yet they are also easy to digest and soothing for the digestive system as they don't have the harsh, scouring qualities of cereal laxatives. The mineral boron that is found in peaches helps stabilize hormones and reduces the craving for something sweet that often occurs as a side-effect of PMS.

PEACHY SALAD

2 large peaches
8 radishes
100g/3½oz French beans
40g/1½oz/⅓ cup hazelnuts
generous handful of mustard
  and cress
2 tsp olive oil
4 tsp orange juice
2 tsp soya sauce

Cut the peaches and radishes into thin slices. Cook the beans in a saucepan of boiling water for 1 minute, then drain. Combine the solid ingredients in a bowl. Mix the oil, juice and soya sauce in a jar and pour over the salad to serve.

900

○ ○ ▽ ⇌ ⊗ ⊗ ⊗

fig

Fibre-rich figs are renowned as laxatives, revitalizing tired digestive systems.

High in natural fruit sugars, figs – particularly dried figs – have a correspondingly high GI but are an extremely worthwhile food to include in a diet plan when eaten in moderation. They are high in fibre and so excellent for digestive health, especially if you suffer from a sluggish digestive system. Figs also make a great occasional snack for dieters, satisfying a sweet tooth without adding any fat.

NUTRIENTS
Vitamin C, beta-carotene, folic acid; calcium, iron, phosphorous, potassium; fibre; tryptophan

Tryptophan, also found in bananas, promotes a good night's sleep.

FIGS WITH PARMA HAM

8 ripe figs
8 slices Parma ham

Slice the figs in two and place on a plate with the Parma ham. Serve with 1 slice of rye, pumpernickel or wholemeal bread per person for a delicious lunch.

007

apple

NUTRIENTS
Vitamin C, beta-carotene, folic acid; calcium, magnesium, phosphorus, potassium; malic acid; pectin

APPLE FACTS
• Apples reduce various forms of inflammation, most notably rheumatism, as well as soothing any inflammation caused by respiratory infection.
• Choose apples that are ripe, avoiding those that are picked early to prolong shelf life – when the fruit won't have developed its optimum nutritional value. Always wash thoroughly, even when buying organic apples.
• Eat apples as soon as possible after purchase and store them somewhere cool and out of direct sunlight.
• When juicing apples, include the skin and the pips – as this is where many of the nutrients are found.

Packed with important vitamins and minerals, as well as fibre, apples are wonderfully cleansing for the whole system – a top food for weight loss.

High in pectin, a soluble fibre that encourages peristalsis (the muscular contractions of the bowel), apples help rid the body of toxins and keep the intestines healthy. Pectin also helps reduce the levels of "bad" LDL cholesterol in the blood.

In addition apples contain enzymes that aid the digestive process, including malic acid which helps to break down and eliminate fatty deposits in the body's cells. Malic acid may assist the body in flushing out toxins that can lead to cellulite.

STUFFED APPLES

4 large sweet apples
8 dried apricots
100g/3½oz/1 cup raisins
400ml/14fl oz/1⅔ cups
**   unsweetened apple juice**

Core the apples and score a shallow cut around the middle of

each so they won't explode in the oven. Place on a shallow baking tray. Chop the apricots, mix with the raisins and place inside the cored apples. Pour the juice over the top and bake in a preheated oven at 180°C/350°F/ Gas Mark 4 for 45 minutes.

Apples are also believed to help relieve many of the symptoms of irritable bowel syndrome that cause discomfort.

For a one-day deep-cleansing programme, eat only apples and drink at least eight large glasses of water. For general daily weight loss, use apples as part of breakfast, chopped into a fruit salad and mixed with some low-fat bio yogurt.

Apples are superb skin-boosters, clearing blemishes and giving a healthy glow.

⬤ ◯ 🍶 ▽ ✪ ✪ ⇔ 🥘 🔪 🔪

apricot

These low-calorie super-sweet fruits make a great snack or can be used to sweeten recipes.

Apricots are very cleansing for the digestive system and encourage detoxification, eliminating the body's waste matter. They are antioxidant, helping the body resist infection and disease. Apricots are mild laxatives, and they are also beneficial for relieving PMS and menstrual cramps.

Dried apricots are a particularly good source of iron.

NUTRIENTS
Vitamins B1, B2, B3, B5, B6, C, beta-carotene, folic acid; calcium, copper, iron, magnesium, potassium, zinc

APRICOT AND BANANA ICE CREAM

2 bananas
6 ripe apricots
500g/1lb 2oz low-fat bio yogurt
1 tsp honey (optional)

Peel the bananas and roughly chop them with the apricots. Blend in a food processor with the yogurt. Add honey to sweeten, if desired. Transfer to a freezerproof container and freeze for 4 hours, stirring occasionally during freezing.

melon

With its high water content, melon moves through the body at great speed, cleansing and rehydrating the system.

Like watermelon, melon has quite a high GI but a low GL score. A slice of melon is a great diet food, nonetheless, and is particularly good at combating bloating and puffiness. Melon's sweet, fragrant juice means it is excellent as a basis for juicing, especially when you use varieties such as Galia and Ogen. And because of its sweetness, melon is a good alternative to biscuits or chocolate for those with sweetness cravings.

NUTRIENTS
Vitamins C, E, beta-carotene, folic acid; calcium, iron, magnesium, phosphorus, potassium, zinc

---

MELON WATERLILY

2 small ripe melons,
 deseeded and peeled
1 cucumber, finely chopped
handful of chopped fresh mint
2 tbsp orange juice

Cut the melon into slices and arrange on a plate like the petals of a waterlily. Scatter over the cucumber and mint, then pour over the juice.

pear

One of the most powerfully cleansing foods around, pears contain pectin, a soluble fibre that keeps the digestive tract healthy.

NUTRIENTS
Vitamin C, beta-carotene, folic acid; calcium, iron, magnesium, phosphorus, potassium, zinc; pectin

Pears are both laxative and diuretic and help to keep your colon in good health. They also have a high iodine content which can aid thyroid function. A "pear-only day" – when you just eat pears and drink eight large glasses of water – is an excellent way to detox and helps control cravings. Pears are available all year round. Team harder varieties with savoury foods and use sweeter, juicier ones for juicing and desserts.

VANILLA PEARS

½ **vanilla pod**
4 **medium pears, peeled, cored and sliced**
20 **sultanas, soaked for 1 hour**
300ml/10½fl oz/1¼ cups water
4 **tbsp low-fat bio yogurt**

Split the vanilla pod down the middle with a sharp knife and remove the black seeds. Use both the seeds and the empty pod in cooking. Place all the ingredients except the yogurt in a saucepan and cook very gently for 20 minutes until the pears are cooked through. Remove the vanilla pod and place the pears on plates. Pour over the juices and serve with the yogurt for a delicious breakfast or supper.

mango

Delicious and deep-cleansing, mangoes are potent detoxifiers.

Supremely cleansing and soothing, mangoes are highly beneficial for the digestive system. They are full of antioxidants, including vitamin E, which is not usually found in fruits, making them one of the most powerful fighters against infection. Mangoes are also top detoxifiers, cleansing the blood and kidneys.

Eating mangoes improves skin and hair condition.

NUTRIENTS
Vitamins B3, C, E, beta-carotene; calcium, iron, magnesium, potassium, zinc; flavonoids

MANGO CHUTNEY

1 ripe mango, peeled and stoned
1 spring onion
1 red pepper, deseeded
1 tbsp chopped flat-leaf parsley
2 tbsp lime juice
2 tbsp olive oil

Finely chop the mango flesh, onion and pepper. Put in a bowl, add the parsley and mix. Pour in the lime juice and oil and leave to marinate for 2 hours. Serve with grilled fish.

banana

Releasing energy over a prolonged period, bananas make an excellent snack for dieters.

For a fruit, the banana is quite high in calories, and its sweetness gives it a high GI rating. However, eaten in moderation it is a good food for dieters because it stabilizes energy levels and lowers harmful LDL cholesterol. Bananas are also an excellent source of low-fat protein, and, with their high fibre content, are deeply cleansing and mildly laxative, too.

NUTRIENTS
Vitamins B6, C, K, beta-carotene, folic acid; calcium, iron, magnesium, phosphorus, potassium, zinc; fibre; protein; tryptophan

NUTTY BANANAS

4 ripe bananas
honey, for rolling
4 tbsp chopped mixed nuts
4 ice-lolly sticks

Peel the bananas and put each one on a stick like a lolly. Roll them lightly in honey and then in nuts. Freeze for 1 hour.

papaya

This sweet, delicious fruit cleanses and soothes the whole digestive tract.

Papayas, or pawpaws, are potent detoxifiers, boosting the immune system and protecting against cardiovascular disease, notably by preventing a build up of plaque on the walls of the blood vessels. They contain papain, an enzyme that digests protein and aids digestion, which in turn may help to encourage weight loss, as well as fibre and high levels of antioxidants to prevent infection and premature ageing.

NUTRIENTS
Vitamin C, beta-carotene; calcium, iron, magnesium, phosphorus, potassium, zinc; papain

TROPICAL FRUIT SALAD

1 papaya, deseeded, peeled and chopped
1 mango, stoned, peeled and chopped
2 slices pineapple, peeled and chopped
2 passion fruit, flesh scooped out
2 tbsp orange juice

Place the first three ingredients in a bowl. Mix the passion fruit flesh with the orange juice. Pour over the fruit salad and serve.

prune

Renowned as natural laxatives, prunes (or dried plums) are good for digestive health.

If you suffer from constipation, prunes are much kinder to the digestive system than "bran-type" cereals, but don't overdo it. When you rebalance your system, you will find that eating plenty, and a wide range, of fresh fruit and vegetables will encourage natural elimination. Prunes also aid liver function and help to lower cholesterol. They are a good source of soluble fibre, which makes you feel full for longer, helping to prevent overeating and weight gain.

NUTRIENTS

Vitamins C, E, beta-carotene, folic acid; calcium, magnesium, phophorus, potassium; fibre

POACHED PRUNES IN FRUIT TEA

2 oranges
2 lemons
2 cinnamon sticks
225g/8oz/1¼ cups stoned prunes
4 fruit tea bags (such as lemon and ginger)

Slice the oranges and lemons into rounds, leaving the skin on. Put in a saucepan with the cinnamon and cover with water. Bring to the boil and simmer to reduce by half. Add the prunes and return to the boil, then remove from the heat. Add the tea bags and leave for 5 minutes. Put the prunes into dessert glasses, strain over the liquid and serve.

cherry

With a low GI and GL rating, a handful of cherries makes an ideal snack for dieters.

Besides being a healthy, low-calorie fruit, cherries have superb powers of detoxification. They contain ellagic acid, a kind of supernutrient that fights cancer, as well as antioxidants that fend off infection. They are particularly beneficial if you have been in a smoky or polluted atmosphere or have consumed more alcohol than you should. Cherries are also antispasmodic and soothing for the digestive tract, especially when combined with yogurt.

NUTRIENTS
Vitamin C, beta-carotene, folic acid; calcium, magnesium, phosphorus, potassium; flavonoids

CHERRY DELIGHT

8 tbsp orange juice
400g/14oz low-fat bio yogurt
400g/14oz cherries, stones
and stalks removed

Stir the orange juice into the yogurt. Pour the mixture over the cherries and serve.

⬩berries

NUTRIENTS

Vitamins C, E, beta-carotene, biotin, folic acid; calcium, iron, magnesium, phosphorus, potassium, sodium

BERRY FACTS

• Raspberries are a mild laxative and beneficial for bloating and other problems associated with PMS. Raspberry leaf tea is recommended for new mothers as it may help the uterus contract.

• Strawberries' antioxidant properties are rejuvenating, especially to the skin, smoothing out lines and wrinkles.

• Both raspberries and strawberries stimulate the circulation of the blood which helps speed up metabolism, so you burn fat more quickly.

• Cranberry juice is very alkaline and so helps to balance an over-acidic system and associated problems, such as heartburn and indigestion. Cranberries are particularly good for the liver, and for urinary and bladder infections.

Full of antioxidants, berries are the dieter's friend – a healthy way to overcome those inevitable cravings for something sweet.

Summer's cornucopia of soft fruits includes strawberries, raspberries, blackberries, blueberries, blackcurrants and redcurrants. They stimulate all of the main organs that are involved in detoxification, boosting metabolism and making the body more efficient at burning fat.

Cranberries are the winter version of these fruits and they also contain powerful antioxidants for cleansing the body.

When you are choosing soft fruit, select berries that are ripe but not over-ripe – so you get maximum sweetness

STRAWBERRIES WITH STRAWBERRY SAUCE

450g/1lb/2⅔ cups strawberries
1 tbsp lemon juice
honey or liqueur (optional)
few fresh mint sprigs

Wash the strawberries and place half of them in a glass dish.

Make the strawberry sauce by puréeing the remainder in a blender with the lemon juice. If this is too tart, add a little honey or a teaspoon of liqueur such as kirsch or framboise. Decorate with sprigs of mint and serve.

without the risk of the fruit going bad before you have time to eat it. To store berries, remove all the packaging, wash throughly and keep in the refrigerator. Eat within one or two days. Leave the fruit to return to room temperature before eating the fruit to taste its full sweetness, and add a little honey or fruit juice if desired.

Many berries are rich in calcium, helping to maintain strong bones and teeth.

orange

High in vitamin C and low in calories, oranges make a perfect healthy snack food at any time.

NUTRIENTS
Vitamin C, beta-carotene, folic acid; calcium, potassium

Packed with the infection-fighting antioxidants beta-carotene and vitamin C, as well as the important minerals potassium and calcium, oranges encourage intestinal health and the elimination of waste and, for this purpose, are best eaten whole and raw. However, when drinking orange juice, it's best to dilute it with the same amount of water as it is acidic and can also cause a surge in blood sugar when drunk neat.

CITRUS BREAKFAST

2 grapefruit
2 oranges
2 mangoes
1 tbsp low-fat bio yogurt/ fromage frais (optional)

Peel all the fruits. Remove the pith from the grapefruit and oranges and slice the flesh into rounds, removing the pips. Cut the mangoes into slices. Place on a plate and add yogurt or fromage frais, if desired.

lemon

This highly astringent, powerful liver cleanser kick-starts the metabolism.

With their high vitamin C and potassium content, lemons offer top protection against infection. They are supremely cleansing for the system, especially the liver, and so make an ideal start to the day: squeeze the juice of one lemon into a cup of hot water and drink first thing. (This should only be tried during detox as excessive lemon can damage tooth enamel.)

NUTRIENTS
Vitamin C; potassium

For added nutrition, try grating the skin and pith of lemons into slow-cooking stews and soups.

LEMONY FRENCH DRESSING

2 tbsp virgin olive oil
juice of 1 lemon
1 clove garlic, crushed
plenty of ground black pepper
pinch of salt

Shake all of the ingredients together in a jar and pour over green or tomato salads. You can add herbs, mustard or a few grains of sugar to vary the flavour. Use sparingly and keep the remaining dressing for use over the next 2 to 3 days.

019

lime

Like all citrus fruits, limes are potent cleansers and are excellent for protecting you from infection while you are losing weight.

Deeply cleansing for the entire digestive system, limes are also particularly effective at fighting off infections such as coughs, colds and sore throats. Squeeze the juice of half a lime into a large bottle of water and sip during the day for added flavour as well as a potent cleanser and hydrator.

NUTRIENTS
Vitamin C, beta-carotene, folic acid; calcium, phosphorus, potassium; bioflavonoids

LIME MARINATED SALMON

50g/1¾oz fresh dill, finely chopped
3 tbsp lime juice
1 tbsp water
1 clove garlic, finely chopped
1 shallot, finely chopped
400g/14oz raw salmon, sliced
½ cucumber, sliced

Place the dill, lime juice, water, garlic and shallot in a jar and shake to mix well. Place the salmon in a dish, pour over the mixture and cover with grease-proof paper. Leave to marinate in the refrigerator for 24 hours. Serve with slices of cucumber.

grapefruit

It's no wonder that grapefruit, low in calories and fat, tremendously tangy and highly detoxifying, is a firm diet-food favourite.

Grapefruits reduce cholesterol, boost energy and immunity, and are very cleansing. Long regarded as the dieter's friend, they are not just low in calories. Recent research has shown that grapefruits can actually speed up weight loss by reducing insulin levels – one of the factors that make us feel hungry – which, in turn, makes us want to eat less.

NUTRIENTS
Vitamins C, E, beta-carotene, folic acid; calcium, copper, magnesium, phosphorus, potassium, zinc; bioflavonoids

CHICORY AND GRAPEFRUIT SALAD

1 grapefruit, halved
250g/9oz chicory, chopped
1 avocado, peeled, stoned
   and chopped
2 tbsp orange juice
2 tsp olive oil
1 tsp soya sauce

Cut half of the grapefruit into small pieces, removing the pith and pips. Mix together with the chicory and avocado in a bowl. Mix together the orange juice, olive oil and soya sauce and the juice from the remaining half of the grapefruit and pour over the salad, adding salt and pepper to taste.

021

sweet potato

NUTRIENTS
Vitamins B6, C, E, beta-carotene, folic acid; calcium, iron, magnesium, phosphorus, potassium; fibre

A delicious and filling diet food, orange-fleshed sweet potatoes have a much lower GI and GL than ordinary white potatoes.

High in fibre, sweet potatoes help promote good digestion. They contain the three main antioxidant vitamins: beta-carotene (which is converted by the body to vitamin A) and vitamins C and E. They are also very energizing, especially when eaten with protein, and they help to eliminate water retention, too.

Sweet potatoes are the highest low-fat source of vitamin E, which is essential for healthy skin.

ROAST SWEET POTATOES

4 sweet potatoes, scrubbed and cubed
2 tbsp olive oil
salt and ground black pepper

Place the sweet potatoes in a baking tray, baste with the olive oil and season. Cook, covered, for 1 hour in a preheated oven at 180°C/ 350°F/Gas Mark 4. Remove from the oven and serve.

carrot

One of the best system cleansers and bursting with nutrients, carrots are a perfect detox food.

Carrots regulate imbalances within your body. They have a particularly powerful cleansing effect on the liver – your most important detoxing organ – which in turn helps your whole system work more efficiently. One of the best ways to eat carrots is raw in salads (their GI levels treble when cooked). Carrot juice also has a high GI, but is nevertheless well worth including in your weight-loss plan – it is one of the best ways of cleansing your whole system during any diet.

NUTRIENTS
Vitamin C, beta-carotene, folic acid; iron, magnesium, potassium, zinc; fibre

CLEANSING CARROT SOUP

450g/1lb carrots
1 medium potato
2 cloves garlic, crushed
55g/2oz parsley
1 tsp sage
1 tsp thyme
1 tbsp vegetable bouillon
¼ tsp cayenne pepper

Scrub and chop the carrots and potato. Bring to the boil in a saucepan with the garlic and 1.2 litres/2 pints/5 cups water. Add the herbs, vegetable bouillon and cayenne and simmer for 25 minutes. Transfer to a food processor and blend until smooth.

onion

Low in calories, onions are fantastically useful in a wide range of dieter's recipes, giving them a real flavour boost.

Onions are great detoxifiers, boosting immunity and cleansing the whole system. They also contain the flavonoid quercetin, an antioxidant that is believed to be key in blocking the formation of cancer cells. Onions are antibiotic and antiseptic and particularly good for the blood, having a thinning effect that prevents clotting, and lowering cholesterol.

NUTRIENTS

Vitamins B1, B6, C, beta-carotene, folic acid; calcium, chlorine, copper, iron, magnesium, phosphorus, potassium, selenium, zinc; quercetin

ONION SOUP

1 tbsp olive oil
450g/1lb onions, chopped
2 cloves garlic, crushed
1 carrot, chopped
1 turnip, chopped
570ml/1 pint/2½ cups
   vegetable bouillon stock
2 tsp soya sauce
2 tbsp chopped flat-leaf
   parsley
1 tbsp sesame seeds

Heat the oil in a saucepan and cook the vegetables very gently for 15 minutes. Add the bouillon and soya sauce, bring to the boil and simmer for 10 minutes. Serve sprinkled with parsley and sesame seeds.

potato

A good source of fibre and vitamin C, potatoes can be a valuable part of your dieting regime.

Although potatoes have a high GI, their GL is generally lower, and boiled or mashed potatoes can make a healthy inclusion in your diet plan when eaten in moderation (just don't add lots of butter to serve). Try combining them with other root vegetables, such as sweet potatoes – roasted in a drizzle of olive oil. But steer clear of chips and potatoes baked in their jackets – they have a GL that is treble that of boiled potatoes.

NUTRIENTS
Vitamins B1, B3, B6, C, folic acid; copper, iron, potassium; fibre

POTATO AND CELERIAC MASH

1 celeriac, peeled and cubed
3 large potatoes, peeled and cubed
knob of low-fat spread
2 tbsp skimmed milk
5 tbsp low-fat bio yogurt
salt and ground black pepper
2 tsp mustard
2 tbsp toasted mixed seeds

Boil the celeriac and potato in a saucepan of water for 10 minutes, then blend in a food processor with all the remaining ingredients, except the seeds. Turn into a serving dish and scatter the seeds over the top to serve.

garlic

Strong in flavour and low in calories, garlic provides the perfect way to pep up sauces and dressings.

This bulb is a fantastic intestinal cleanser and helps purify the liver, too. Taken on a regular basis, garlic builds immune health and is naturally antibiotic, antibacterial and antiviral. It also promotes heart health and good circulation. Garlic's distinctive flavour makes it invaluable in cooking. Use it to add bite to stir-fries, sauces, salads and dressings. You can also roast a whole garlic in the oven and serve it as a vegetable – delicious.

NUTRIENTS

Vitamins B6, C, folic acid; calcium, iron, magnesium, phosphorus, potassium, zinc; amino acids

AÏOLI (GARLIC MAYONNAISE)

2 medium free-range eggs
4 tbsp lemon juice
3–4 cloves garlic, crushed
300ml/½ pint/1¼ cups olive oil
1 tsp mustard
salt and ground black pepper
2 tbsp boiling water

Beat the eggs with the lemon juice in a food processor. Stir in the garlic, then add the oil very gradually, mixing all the time. When smooth, stir in the mustard and season to taste. Beat in the boiling water to stabilize.

leek

A member of the onion family, the leek is a powerful antioxidant and potent cleanser.

Packed with nutrients, leeks are excellent for fighting off infection and disease as well as cleansing the body. They also energize the immune and nervous systems. Good diuretics, leeks help reduce water retention and bloating, and they are also beneficial for inflammatory conditions, especially arthritis.

NUTRIENTS
Vitamins C, E, K, beta-carotene, biotin, folic acid; calcium, iron, magnesium, phosphorus, potassium, zinc; fibre

LEEK AND CARROT SOUP

1 large potato, scrubbed and chopped
450g/1lb carrots, scrubbed and chopped
450g/1lb leeks, washed and sliced
1 tbsp olive oil
1.2 litres/2 pints/5 cups vegetable bouillon stock or vegetable stock
salt and ground black pepper

In a large saucepan, sweat the vegetables in the oil, stirring constantly for 2 minutes. Add the stock and bring to the boil. Simmer, covered, for 15 minutes, add the seasoning and blend in a food processor.

027

celeriac

Celeriac, or celery root, is an excellent diuretic, reducing water retention and bloating.

NUTRIENTS
Vitamin C; calcium, iron, magnesium, potassium, phosphorus; fibre

A versatile yet often neglected vegetable, celeriac has recently become more widely available. It reduces high blood pressure, removes excess acid and also regulates the nervous and lymphatic systems. Celeriac can be used raw and cooked – it has a deliciously nutty flavour and is very good mashed and mixed with other root vegetables such as carrots and potatoes.

Celeriac soothes arthritis inflammation and promotes kidney health.

CELERIAC SALAD

2 small celeriacs
juice of 1 lemon
115g/4oz toasted mixed seeds
8 tbsp low-fat bio yogurt
2 tbsp mustard

Peel the celeriac and chop into matchsticks. Pour over the lemon juice immediately to stop discolouration. Mix with the remaining ingredients, season to taste and serve.

radish

Packed with nutrients, the peppery radish adds spice to salads and speeds up metabolism.

Radishes increase the production of digestive juices so that the body breaks down and metabolizes food more efficiently – especially when they are eaten with starches. They have a deeply cleansing effect, particularly on the respiratory system, and help to fight off infection. Radishes also contain high levels of zinc, one of the most important antioxidant minerals.

NUTRIENTS
Vitamins B, C, beta-carotene, folic acid; calcium, iron, magnesium, phosphorus, potassium, sodium, zinc

Eating radishes can help clear sinuses and sore throats.

CASHEW DIP WITH RADISH CRUDITÉS

225g/8oz/1¼ cups cashew nuts
4 tsp chopped marjoram
4 tsp shoyu
2 bunches radishes, trimmed
2 red peppers, deseeded and sliced
4 sticks celery, trimmed

Grind the cashews in a food processor, adding water to form a thick cream. Mix in the flavourings and transfer to a dish. Serve with the crudités.

tomato

NUTRIENTS

Vitamins C, E, biotin, beta-carotene, folic acid; calcium, chlorine, magnesium, potassium, sodium, zinc

TOMATO FACTS

• Tomatoes cleanse and soothe the liver, the body's principal organ of detoxification.

• Lycopene, an antioxidant found in large quantities in cooked tomatoes, is thought to be particularly useful in the prevention of prostate cancer.

• The salicylates that are contained in tomatoes, and have many health benefits for adults, may increase hyperactivity in children already affected with the condition.

• Tomatoes should be avoided by anyone who suffers from inflammatory conditions such as osteoarthritis, and in some cases people who have asthma or bronchitis.

Made up of 90 percent water, tomatoes are wonderfully hydrating, as well as delicious and versatile, plus they have a low GI and GL and a very low calorie count – perfect for dieters!

Although they are actually fruits, most people think of tomatoes as vegetables. They play a major part in the Mediterranean diet – noted for its success in weight loss and heart health, despite its inclusion of rich foods. This is partly because tomatoes are rich in salicylates, naturally occurring compounds that are associated with lowered risk of heart disease.

FIERY TOMATO SAUCE

1 tsp olive oil
2 cloves garlic, crushed
1 chilli pepper, deseeded and chopped
1kg/2lbs 4oz tomatoes, skinned and roughly chopped
pinch of salt, to taste
2–4 tbsp low-fat bio yogurt, to taste

Heat the olive oil in a frying pan and lightly cook the garlic and chilli, then gradually add the tomatoes and cook over a medium heat for 10 minutes. Add salt and plenty of yogurt to make a creamy sauce. (The more yogurt you add, the less fiery the sauce will be.) Serve with al dente wholegrain pasta.

Their high water content hydrates the digestive system and improves its function, especially when they are eaten raw. They also contain all the antioxidant vitamins – C and E and beta-carotene, plus the mineral zinc, fortifying the immune system against ageing and infection and lowering the risk of disease.

red pepper

NUTRIENTS
Vitamins B, C, E, beta-carotene, folic acid; calcium, iron, magnesium, potassium, zinc; fibre

ROASTED PEPPERS

3 large red peppers
1 tbsp olive oil
15g/½oz basil leaves

Brush the peppers with the oil, sprinkle with basil and a little salt and roast in a preheated oven at 190°C/375°F/Gas Mark 5 for 1½ hours until blackened. Remove from the oven. When cool, peel off the skin, discard the stem, core and seeds and cut into quarters.

Stimulating and invigorating for the digestion and circulation, red peppers are top metabolism-boosters, helping the body to burn fat.

Bursting with antioxidants, particularly vitamin C and beta-carotene, red peppers fight infection and disease. They normalize blood pressure and also help combat stress, owing to their high vitamin C and magnesium contents, which support the immune system and adrenal glands. They are especially beneficial for dieters when eaten raw or taken as a juice.

avocado

Creamy and versatile, packed with nutrients and healthy fats, avocado is a delicious diet food.

Avocado is often avoided by dieters because of its high calorie count, but most of its fats are beneficial ones: it is particularly high in omega-6 fatty acids (linoleic acid) that stabilize blood sugar levels and keep hunger at bay. Avocado also helps to decrease the acid overload found in most diets and is a rich source of the antioxidant vitamin E, which works especially well when combined with selenium (found in sesame seeds).

NUTRIENTS
Vitamins B1, B2, B3, B5, C, E, K, folic acid; copper, iron, phosphorus, potassium, zinc; fibre; omega-6 fatty acids

BACON AND AVOCADO SALAD

8 rashers lean bacon, diced
2 tbsp olive oil
2 avocados, stoned and sliced
2 hard-boiled free-range
   eggs, shelled and chopped
large handful of rocket
handful of toasted mixed
   seeds
large handful of chopped
   mixed herbs
juice of 2 lemons

Fry the bacon in half of the oil. Put in a bowl with the avocado flesh, eggs, rocket, seeds and herbs. Mix the remaining oil with the lemon juice and season to taste. Pour over the salad, toss and serve.

beetroot

NUTRIENTS
Vitamins B3, B6, C, beta-carotene, folic acid; calcium, iron, magnesium, phosphorus, potassium, zinc; fibre

Deliciously sweet and low in calories, fresh beetroot is also a powerful detoxifier.

Revered in Eastern Europe for its blood-purifying properties, beetroot is one of the great cleansers, especially of the liver, intestines, kidneys and gall bladder. It also stimulates the circulatory system, speeding up metabolism. The high amount of fibre contained in beetroot improves digestive health, aiding the absorption of food and helping to regulate processes within the body – two key factors in successful weight loss. This nutrient-rich vegetable also makes an excellent detox juice, especially when mixed with carrot, spinach and cabbage.

ROASTED BEETROOT

4 medium beetroots, washed (unpeeled)
1 tbsp olive oil
1 tsp sea salt

Brush the beetroots with a little olive oil, sprinkle with salt and roast in a preheated oven at 180°C/350°F/Gas Mark 4 for about 1 hour (depending on size). When cooked, a skewer or knife tip will easily slice into the flesh. The roasted beetroots will serve 4 as an accompaniment or 2 when sliced over a green salad.

cucumber

Made up of 96 percent water, cucumbers are wonderfully cleansing and beneficial to dieters.

With its high water content, cucumber is a good cleanser for the whole system, facilitating the digestive process, and an excellent diuretic and a mild laxative. It also helps flush out both the kidneys and bladder, helping prevent water retention as well as dissolving the uric acid that can cause bladder infections and cystitis. Cucumber is very versatile. Use it as a crudité, in salads, sandwiches and in vegetable juices.

NUTRIENTS
Vitamin C, beta-carotene, folic acid; calcium, iron, potassium, silica, zinc

CUCUMBER YOGURT CHEESE

200g/7oz low-fat soft white cheese
55g/2oz low-fat bio yogurt
¼ tsp lemon juice
¼ tsp olive oil
1 clove garlic, crushed
salt and ground black pepper
400g/14oz cucumbers, diced

Place the cheese, yogurt, lemon juice, olive oil, garlic and seasoning in a bowl and whip together into a smooth cream. Add the cucumber and serve in a glass dish as a dip for vegetable crudités.

courgette

High in fibre, courgettes encourage a healthy digestive system, lower cholesterol and generally detoxify the body.

Belonging to the same family as marrow, squash and pumpkin, courgettes are mildly laxative and diuretic as well as being gentle on the digestive system. They are very filling – keeping hunger pangs at bay – and alkaline, counteracting the generally high acid levels in most peoples' diets and soothing the liver, helping the body's metabolism to function efficiently.

PRAWN STUFFED COURGETTES

8 small courgettes, blanched
1 onion, chopped
1 clove garlic, chopped
1 tbsp olive oil
4 tomatoes, chopped
2 drops Tabasco
1 tsp thyme
250g/9oz cooked prawns, peeled

Halve the courgettes lengthways, scoop out the flesh and chop. Fry the onion and garlic in the oil. Add the tomatoes, courgette flesh and flavourings and simmer for 10 minutes. Add the prawns. Pour into the courgette shells and bake, covered, in a preheated oven at 220°C/425°F/Gas Mark 7 for 15 minutes.

mushroom

A fantastic slow-release energy food, mushrooms thin the blood, improving circulation and the rate at which you burn fat.

Releasing energy into the body over a prolonged period, without upsetting blood sugar levels, mushrooms help stave off hunger pangs. They are also a good source of zinc, supporting the immune system. Many varieties of mushroom are available and you can use them all in any recipe, including substituting oriental varieties, such as shiitake and maiitake.

NUTRIENTS
Vitamins B3, B5, folic acid; calcium, iron, zinc

MUSHROOM AND MANGETOUT SOUP

2 tbsp wholemeal or
  buckwheat flour
1.2 litres/2 pints/5 cups water
1 clove garlic, crushed
1 tsp dried thyme
1 tbsp olive oil
175g/6oz mushrooms, sliced
175g/6oz mangetout, sliced
55g/2oz parsley, chopped
2 tbsp vegetable bouillon

In a saucepan, make a smooth paste of the flour and a little water. Add the garlic and thyme, then heat slowly, adding the water and olive oil gradually, stirring continuously. Add the remaining ingredients and bring to the boil. Cover and simmer for 20 minutes, then blend in a food processor until smooth.

broccoli

NUTRIENTS
Vitamins B2, B3, B5, C,
beta-carotene, folic acid; calcium,
iron, magnesium, phosphorus,
potassium, zinc; fibre

BROCCOLI FACTS
• Both green and purple sprouting
broccoli contain a wide range of
nutrients. Always look for broccoli
with a good strong colour and
avoid any that is starting to turn
yellow or wilt. Eat broccoli within
a day or two of purchase and store
in a refrigerator.
• Broccoli is a good source of folic
acid – levels of which are often
reduced by taking the contraceptive
pill, which can result in anaemia.
• Folic acid also promotes the
production of serotonin, a mood-
lifting chemical that is produced
naturally within the body.
• Broccoli should be cooked for as
short a time as possible – ideally
just a few minutes. Steaming is the
best method, followed by boiling in
a small amount of water.

Gram for gram, this powerhouse of nutrients has
half the fibre of wholemeal bread but only a tenth
of its calories.

High in both antioxidants and fibre, broccoli is a deeply
cleansing vegetable of both the entire digestive system and the
liver, the body's most important organ of detoxification. This
has a beneficial effect on dieting as, when the liver is working
to its full potential, the whole body functions better, enabling
you to absorb and use nutrients from food and eliminate waste
effectively, and preventing the build up of toxins and the
storage of fat.

BROCCOLI RISOTTO

1 tbsp olive oil
1 large onion, chopped
1 clove garlic, chopped
100g/3½oz/½ cup brown rice
2 tbsp vegetable bouillon
175g/6oz broccoli, cut into florets

Heat the oil in a large saucepan
and gently fry the onion and

garlic. Stir in the rice and cover
with twice its volume of water.
Add the vegetable bouillon. Cook
for about 30 minutes (check the
packet instructions). Add the
broccoli florets and cook for
a further 5 minutes. Season
to taste and serve with a fish
or meat dish.

Broccoli contains a range of B vitamins, including B2 which benefits skin, hair and nails, and combines powerfully with B5 to metabolize fats into energy.

This truly miraculous vegetable is profoundly strengthening for the immune system and is now known to help prevent bowel cancer. This is because it contains sulfuraphane, a substance which detoxifies and effectively secretes the carcinogens we are breathing in and eating all the time.

Tenderstem broccoli is particularly rich in antioxidant sulfuraphanes.

globe artichoke

Not to be confused with the root Jerusalem artichokes, globe artichokes are fantastic diuretics.

Superb liver cleansers, globe artichokes also lower cholesterol and stimulate the gall bladder, and they contain inulin which supports healthy bacteria in the gut. They also help banish cellulite, especially when used as a juice mixed with yellow peppers and parsley.

NUTRIENTS
Vitamins B3, C, K, beta-carotene, folic acid; calcium, iron, magnesium, phosphorus, potassium, sodium; fibre; inulin

ARTICHOKES WITH LEMON

4 globe artichokes, washed
2 tsp wholegrain mustard
juice of 2 lemons
2 tbsp olive oil

Remove the artichokes' stalks and trim the bases so they will sit upright. Trim the points off the leaves. Boil in a large pan of water for 30–40 minutes. When cool enough to handle, pull out the soft inner leaves and remove the fibrous choke with a teaspoon. In a jug, mix the mustard, lemon juice and oil and season to taste.
Pour into the centre of the artichokes and serve.

asparagus

A powerful stimulant for the kidneys and liver, asparagus acts on water retention and bloating.

One of the delights of summer, asparagus should always be bought fresh and cooked lightly for maximum flavour and nutrition. It is an excellent slow-release energy food, helping to stabilize blood sugar levels which, in turn, keeps hunger pangs and food cravings at bay. Asparagus is also mildly laxative and helps to reduce inflammation.

NUTRIENTS
Vitamins C, K, beta-carotene, folic acid; phosphorus, potassium, zinc; fibre

ASPARAGUS AND NEW POTATOES

225g/8oz new potatoes
10 asparagus spears, trimmed
1 tsp olive oil
¼ tsp dried chilli flakes
½ tsp grated Parmesan cheese

Boil the new potatoes in a saucepan of water until just tender and steam the asparagus for 10 minutes. In another pan, gently heat the olive oil and fry the chilli flakes for 2 minutes, then add the potatoes and let them absorb the chilli-flavoured oil for 2 minutes, shaking the pan regularly. Transfer to a bowl with the asparagus, season with salt if necessary, mix in the Parmesan and serve.

chicory

Also known as Belgian endive, chicory is very low in calories and has an interesting bitter taste.

NUTRIENTS
Vitamin B1, beta-carotene, folic acid; iron, phosphorus, potassium, zinc; fibre

Packed with fibre, chicory promotes the elimination of waste from the body, ensuring good digestive health. It also contains important immune-boosting vitamins and minerals, including vitamin B1, which increases energy levels, making it a good mid-morning or mid-afternoon snack with a low-fat dip.

ROASTED CHICORY WITH WALNUTS

4 heads chicory, cut in half
2 tbsp olive oil
salt and ground black pepper
4 tbsp chopped walnuts

Place the chicory in an ovenproof dish, pour over the oil, season and roast in a preheated oven at 180°C/350°F/Gas Mark 4 for 20 minutes. Scatter the walnuts over and serve as a side dish to fish.

spinach

This delicious leafy green is a wonderful slow-release energy food, keeping hunger at bay.

A natural laxative, spinach aids liver function, neutralizing the toxins present in our bodies. The B vitamins found in spinach strengthen the immune system, fighting off infection, and boost energy levels to fight long-term fatigue and stress. Its high potassium content regulates blood-fat levels.

NUTRIENTS
Vitamins B2, B3, B6, C, K, beta-carotene, folic acid; calcium, iron, magnesium, potassium, zinc; fibre

The oxalic acid contained in spinach can exacerbate kidney or bladder stones.

SPINACH SOUP

1 tbsp olive oil
1.5kg/3lb 5oz spinach, washed
6 sticks celery, sliced
2 heaped tbsp vegetable bouillon
1 heaped tbsp fresh herbs (tarragon, thyme)
1 tsp grated nutmeg
4 tbsp low-fat bio yogurt

Heat the oil in a large saucepan and sauté the spinach until just tender. Barely cover with water, add the remaining ingredients, except for the yogurt, and simmer for 10 minutes. Blend in a food processor until smooth and serve with a spoonful of yogurt.

watercress

NUTRIENTS

Vitamins B3, B6, C, E, K, beta-carotene, folic acid; calcium, copper, iodine, iron, magnesium, phosphorous, potassium, zinc; fibre; glucosinolates

WATERCRESS FACTS

• Watercress is well known for its therapeutic effects on the skin, combating inflammatory problems, such as eczema and psoriasis, and as a folk remedy for freckles and spots.

• Unlike in spinach, the zinc found in watercress is free of oxalic acid, so it is suitable for people with kidney or bladder stones. In fact, it helps to dissolve such stones.

• Watercress lowers cholesterol and raises energy levels and is particularly useful for those suffering from stress or with a suppressed immune system.

• You can add watercress in small quantities to vegetable juices – it goes well with carrot-based blends. But don't overdo it or its peppery taste will bring tears to your eyes!

An outstanding diet food, watercress is a powerful antioxidant that cleanses the kidneys and bladder, purifies the blood and increases energy levels.

Watercress possesses potent health benefits, increased by the fact that it is almost invariably eaten raw. It has very high levels of vitamins and negligible calories, and acts as a tonic on the digestive system, improving nutrient absorption from other foods and speeding up metabolism to reduce absorption of fat.

Mildly diuretic and laxative, this peppery salad leaf stimulates the liver, gall bladder, pancreas, kidneys and bladder, regulating bodily processes essential for weight management.

APRICOT AND WATERCRESS SALAD

2 bunches watercress, washed and trimmed
55g/2oz/⅓ cup dried apricots
2 punnets salad cress, cut and washed
2 tsp olive oil
2 tsp white wine vinegar
2 spring onions, finely chopped

4 tsp finely chopped fresh coriander

Put the first three ingredients in a bowl. Make a dressing from the remaining ingredients, shaking well in a jar to mix. Pour over the salad and serve.

Its high iodine content aids thyroid function and improves metabolism. Watercress is also rich in folic acid which strengthens the nervous system and blood cells of mother and child during pregnancy and reduces the risk of birth defects in unborn babies. Its high levels of antioxidants, glucosinolates and phagocytes (detoxifying white blood cells) boost the immune system, increasing resistance to infection and disease.

cabbage

A powerful detoxifier, cabbage is extremely cleansing for the digestive system, in particular the stomach and upper colon.

Famous as the basis of a dieter's soup owing to its low calories and low fat content, cabbage is especially beneficial for sufferers of constipation as it encourages contractions of the bowel and also prevents the auto-intoxication that can occur when waste is re-absorbed into the system. The highest concentration of nutrients is in green cabbage – but red and white are good for you, too, especially when eaten raw in salads.

NUTRIENTS

Vitamins C, E, K, beta-carotene, folic acid; calcium, iodine, iron, magnesium, phosphorus, zinc; fibre

RED CABBAGE SLAW

500g/1lb 2oz red cabbage, finely shredded
1 red onion, finely sliced
2 carrots, cut into matchsticks
1 fennel bulb, shredded
2 tbsp chopped flat-leaf parsley
6 tbsp low-fat bio yogurt
1 tbsp white wine vinegar
2 tsp Dijon mustard
1 tsp honey (optional)
1 clove garlic, crushed
salt and ground black pepper

Put all the vegetables, together with the parsley, into a bowl and mix well. For the dressing, mix together the remaining ingredients. Pour over the salad, toss well and serve.

kale

Belonging to the same family as cabbage, kale is a highly nutritious diet food.

Kale (sometimes known as curly kale) contains high levels of beta-carotene, which is converted by the body into vitamin A, boosting the immune system, protecting and strengthening the respiratory and digestive systems and building strong teeth, hair and bones. It is very good for the skin, both in cases of eczema and dermatitis and also as a means of improving the complexion. Kale contains high levels of water, making it a useful digestive aid and superb diet food, and its glucosinolate content stimulates detoxification.

NUTRIENTS
Vitamins B2, B3, C, E, K, beta-carotene, folic acid; iron, magnesium, zinc; fibre; glucosinolates

SEEDY KALE

1 head kale
1 tsp olive oil
2 tbsp toasted mixed seeds
salt and ground black pepper

Wash and shred the kale. Heat the oil in a large saucepan, add the kale, cover and cook over a low heat until tender. Season to taste and stir in the seeds. Serve as an accompaniment to meat or fish dishes.

aubergine

NUTRIENTS
Beta-carotene, folic acid; iron, phosphorus; fibre

AUBERGINE PÂTÉ

2 aubergines
1 clove garlic, crushed
2 tsp lemon juice
2 tsp olive oil
salt and ground black pepper
2 tbsp chopped flat-leaf
   parsley

Prick the aubergine skin several times, cut in two and bake (flesh-side down) on a lightly greased baking sheet for 30 minutes in a preheated oven at 190°C/375°F/Gas Mark 5. Discard the skin and blend in a food processor with the remaining ingredients. Serve as a dip with crudités, oatcakes or rye bread.

The versatile aubergine adds a deliciously smoky flavour to a wide variety of dishes and can also make a tasty, diet-friendly snack.

Because aubergines are generally fried in thin slices, absorbing massive amounts of oil, they are often shunned by dieters. But if you cut them in half and bake them using only a little oil you will reduce the fat content while keeping their distinctive taste. Aubergines belong to the nightshade family and should be avoided by anyone suffering from osteoarthritis as they may increase inflammation.

lettuce

Highly diuretic, lettuce is an excellent choice for those suffering from water retention and bloating.

Thanks to its negligible calories, lettuce is well known as a diet food, but it has much more to it than that. Rich in antioxidant vitamin C and beta-carotene, lettuce encourages good health while you lose weight and, combined with the silicon also found in the vegetable, supports bones and connective tissue.

NUTRIENTS
Vitamins B, C, beta-carotene, folic acid; calcium, copper, iron, magnesium, phosphorus, potassium, zinc; silicon

CHILLED LETTUCE AND AVOCADO SOUP

250g/9oz low-fat bio yogurt
1 ripe avocado, peeled and
  stoned
juice of 1 lemon
1 crisp lettuce
2 tbsp chives
salt and ground black pepper

In a food processor, blend together the yogurt, avocado and lemon juice and gradually add water until the mixture has the consistency of milk. Add the lettuce and chives and process until the mixture is smooth. Season to taste and serve chilled.

nettle

NUTRIENTS
Vitamins B1, B2, B3, B5, C, K,
beta-carotene; calcium, iron,
magnesium, potassium

Used for centuries as a blood purifier, nettle is a potent liver cleanser.

This stinging plant has powerful diuretic properties, making it an excellent remedy for bloating and water retention. Nettle also stimulates liver function, ridding the body of toxins, and improves circulation, so regulating metabolism. High in antioxidants, it boosts immunity, too. The best way to use nettle is as a tea. Take care when picking and handling the fresh plant – don't touch it without gloves until it has been boiled.

Nettle tea is particularly beneficial for relieving gout and arthritis.

NETTLE TEA

4 fresh nettles
½ lemon or lime

Cut off the tips (top 7.5cm/ 3in) of the nettles, wash them and place in a teapot. Add the lemon or lime, cover in boiling water and allow to steep for 5–10 minutes before drinking.

sorrel

A traditional remedy for digestive problems, this sharp-tasting salad leaf is making a comeback.

NUTRIENTS
Vitamin C, beta-carotene, folic acid; iron

Sorrel has a strong lemony taste and combines well with other salad leaves – adding bite to salad dishes. Like other dark leafy greens, it is packed with vitamin C and iron. Used in soups and sauces, it is a good immunity booster, building up your resistance to infection while you diet.

Use garden sorrel (*Rumex scutatus*) rather than the more acidic wild sorrel (*Rumex acetosa*).

SORREL SALAD

225g/8oz sorrel leaves
225g/8oz lamb's lettuce
225g/8oz cherry tomatoes
2 tsp olive oil
4 tsp white wine vinegar
2 cloves garlic, finely chopped
4 tsp chopped fresh herbs

Wash the salad leaves and tear into strips. Put in a bowl with the tomatoes. To make the dressing, mix the remaining ingredients in a jar, shaking well, and season to taste. Pour over the salad, toss and serve.

⬤ ⬤ 🥤 ▽ ✪ ✦ ⟺ 🥦 🔪 ⌀

celery

NUTRIENTS
Vitamins B3, C, E, beta-carotene, folic acid; calcium, potassium, sodium; fibre

CELERY JUICE

2 small bunches watercress
head of celery
2 yellow peppers, deseeded

Wash all the vegetables and cut them into juicer-size pieces, then juice in a juicer. Stir and drink immediately.

Extremely low in calories and excellent for fighting fluid retention, this classic diet food is also highly cleansing and promotes kidney function.

Fresh, crunchy celery has earned its reputation as a first-rate diet food owing to the fact that it takes more calories to eat and digest than it actually contains. However, it has more to offer in the diet and nutritional stakes than being low in calories.

Introducing plenty of celery into your diet can reduce your intake of salt. This is because celery has a deliciously salty taste and so can be added to dishes as a healthy substitute for salt itself. Most people's diets are generally too high in salt which upsets the body's water, potassium and sodium balance, leading to fluid retention – the dieter's enemy – as well as to increased blood pressure. Celery also helps to build red blood cells, important for removing waste from the body.

Mix celery with watercress and yellow pepper for an excellent breakfast juice that is truly cleansing, improving circulation and lowering blood pressure (see recipe opposite). Or try juicing with tomato – a virtuous Bloody Mary!

CELERY FACTS

• Celery has a soothing quality and is very beneficial in times of stress.
• The ancient Greeks used the leaves of celery as laurels to decorate their renowned athletes, while the ancient Romans used celery as a seasoning.
• Celery is cooling in hot weather.
• Raw celery has been used only relatively recently. Until the seventeenth century, it was used solely as a medicine when it was cooked before serving.

fennel

A fabulous fat digester, fennel stimulates metabolism and regulates blood-fat levels.

NUTRIENTS
Vitamins B6, C, folic acid; calcium, iron, magnesium, phosphorus, potassium, zinc; fibre; phytoestrogens

With its distinctive aniseed flavour, fennel perks up any dish and also makes a very cleansing juice, particularly for the liver and digestive system. It is a good skin cleanser, too. Fennel is an excellent diuretic and helps break down fat, releasing the water that is stored in fat cells in the body.

BAKED FENNEL

**4 fennel bulbs
juice of 2 lemons
4 tbsp olive oil**

Trim the fennel and cut into quarters. Put in a baking dish, pour over the lemon juice and olive oil and season to taste. Bake in a preheated oven at 180°C/350°F/Gas Mark 4 for 45 minutes. Serve with fish.

seaweed

Seaweed and sea vegetables contain excellent levels of iodine – an essential mineral that assists thyroid function, keeping the body's metabolism working at optimum levels.

Seaweed is an extremely effective detoxifier that removes dangerous heavy metals from the system. Its high mineral content helps to keep blood pressure under control, supports the kidneys and nervous system, promotes cellular growth and the formation of red blood cells and increases your immunity to infection. Use in soups or dried as a garnish.

NUTRIENTS

B vitamins; calcium, copper, iodine, iron, magnesium, phosphorus, potassium, zinc; protein; silicon

BEAN AND SEAWEED BROTH

225g/8oz mixed dried beans
115g/4oz/½ cup pearl barley
1 onion, sliced
1 carrot, sliced
2 sticks celery, sliced
55g/2oz spinach
55g/2oz dulse seaweed
1 tbsp miso
¼ tsp sage
1 tsp cumin
1.2 litres/2 pints/5 cups water
115g/4oz low-fat bio yogurt

Soak the beans and barley overnight. Next day, put all ingredients, except the yogurt, in a saucepan and bring to the boil. Simmer, covered, for 45 minutes. Serve with the yogurt.

bulgur wheat

A light, nutty-tasting cracked wheat grain, bulgur is a great complex carbohydrate and fantastic source of dietary fibre.

Bulgur wheat has been cracked, roasted and steamed before it is sold and the result is a deliciously nutty flavour. It is rich in fibre, boosting digestion, and is a slow-release energy food that stabilizes blood sugars and prevents food cravings. It also helps to lower cholesterol levels and protect against infection.

NTRIENTS

Vitamins B1, B2, B3; copper, iron, magnesium, phosphorus; fibre; protein

TABBOULEH

225g/8oz/1 cup bulgur wheat
pinch of salt
1 cucumber, sliced
4 spring onions, chopped
4 tomatoes, chopped
8 tbsp chopped fresh parsley
2 tbsp olive oil
2 tsp lemon juice

Cover the bulgur wheat with boiling water (about 125ml/4fl oz/½ cup) and leave to stand for 30 minutes. When cool, mix in the cucumber, onions, tomatoes, parsley, olive oil and lemon juice. Add salt and pepper to taste. For a variation, you can add a few prawns.

rye

This high-energy grain is extremely cleansing for the whole system and in particular the liver.

Rye, like oats, is often tolerated by people who can't eat wheat. It has more fibre and less gluten and is very filling, making it an excellent choice for those who feel hungry all the time. Rye bread sandwiches make a particularly good lunch for dieters as the slow release of energy from the grain helps to stave off mid-afternoon hunger pangs or food cravings.

NUTRIENTS
Vitamins B1, B2, B3, B5, B6, B9, B12, E; calcium, iron, magnesium, manganese, phosphorus, potassium, zinc; fibre; protein

SARDINE SARNIES

225g/8oz canned sardines
2 spring onions
2 tbsp lemon juice
2 tbsp chopped parsley
black pepper, to taste
8 slices rye bread

Mash the sardines with the next four ingredients in a bowl, using a fork. Place on the slices of rye bread and serve with a watercress salad.

oats

NUTRIENTS
Vitamins B1, B2, B3, B5, E, folic acid; calcium, iron, magnesium, phosphorus, selenium, silica; fibre; protein

BIRCHER-BENNER MUESLI

8 tbsp porridge oats
8 tbsp raisins or sultanas
8 tbsp apple or pineapple juice
2 apples or pears
4 tbsp chopped mixed nuts
1 tsp ground ginger
2 tsp honey (optional)
8 tbsp low-fat bio yogurt

Soak the oats and raisins or sultanas overnight in the juice. Next morning, grate the apples or pears and mix into the oats together with the nuts, ginger and honey, if desired. Pour the yogurt on top and serve. For a variation, mix in any other chopped fruits of your choice.

One of the most nutritious grains, oats are full of protein and minerals and contain a soluble fibre that helps the digestive system to work at an optimum level.

Oats reduce the absorption of carbohydrates into the blood stream, stabilizing blood sugar levels and combating food cravings and hunger pangs. They also help alleviate mood swings – particularly those associated with PMS as oats stabilize oestrogen levels – and reduce water retention.

The soluble fibre found in oats lowers cholesterol and blood pressure, boosting cardiovascular health. Oats may also stimulate the thyroid gland which produces the hormones that regulate the body's metabolizing of food into energy.

By providing dietary bulk, oats improve the digestive process, preventing or easing constipation. At the same time, they are soothing for the digestive tract, especially for conditions such as gastritis and irritable bowel syndrome, and, because they sweep food and carcinogens through the gut, they may help to prevent bowel cancer.

Always choose rolled oats and oatmeal rather than any of the instant varieties for making porridge (a superb breakfast for dieters when made with skimmed milk) as they have not been through any refining processes and so haven't lost any of their nutritional properties. They can be eaten raw or cooked, and oatcakes make a perfect snack for dieters. Oats are often a good substitute for those with an intolerance to wheat. However, sufferers from coeliac disease should avoid any gluten and so cannot eat oats, barley or rye as well as wheat.

OAT FACTS
• Oats are renowned for their tranquillizing and relaxing effects – a folk remedy for insomnia advises sleeping on a pillow filled with oats.
• Oats help to build strong bones, teeth and connective tissue and are good for convalescence, especially after childbirth as they may help to tone the uterus.

wild rice

NUTRIENTS
Vitamin E; iodine, potassium, selenium; fibre; protein; tryptophan

High in fibre and protein while low in fat, wild rice is not a rice at all, but a grain, *Zizania aquatica*.

Wild rice has a delicate, nutty flavour and can be served alone or with brown rice. It is an excellent source of fibre and protein and also contains the amino acid tryptophan. This is a natural sedative – useful for anyone with trouble sleeping – and a natural mood enhancer. Raising tryptophan levels helps to alleviate symptoms of depression, anxiety and PMS.

PRAWN RISOTTO

2 tbsp olive oil
2 handfuls finely chopped vegetables (such as peppers, fennel, celery, courgettes, carrots)
115g/4oz/⅔ cups wild rice
115g/4oz/⅔ cups brown rice
250g/9oz cooked prawns, peeled
2 heaped tbsp chopped fresh herbs (such as parsley, coriander, basil, tarragon)
salt and ground black pepper

Heat 1 tbsp of the oil in a saucepan and gently fry the vegetables for 10 minutes. In another pan, heat the remaining oil and gently fry the rice for 2 minutes. Add 300ml/10½fl oz/ 1¼ cups boiling water, bring to the boil and simmer until tender (check the cooking times on the individual packets). Add the herbs and seasoning, stir in the vegetables and prawns and serve.

brown rice

Brown rice is a much better choice for dieters than its white counterpart – its slow-release carbs stabilize blood sugar and help banish cravings.

A good source of protein and dietary fibre, brown rice is an excellent cleanser and regulator of the digestive tract. It also reduces water retention and other side-effects of PMS such as breast tenderness, and it's loaded with immune-boosting B vitamins. But the benefits don't stop there: not only is brown rice far more nutritious than white, it's also very fillling, so you need only relatively small portions compared to white rice.

NUTRIENTS
Vitamins B3, B5, B6, folic acid; calcium, iron, magnesium, manganese, phosphorus, potassium, zinc; fibre; protein

KEDGEREE

350g/12oz smoked haddock
1 tbsp olive oil
1 onion, finely chopped
½ tsp ground coriander
½ tsp ground cumin
1 tsp ground turmeric
¼ tsp cayenne pepper
100g/3½oz/½ cup brown rice
2 tbsp chopped fresh flat-leaf parsley

Poach the haddock in boiling water for 15 minutes, drain and flake. Heat the oil in a large pan and fry the onion and spices. Add the rice and 400ml/14fl oz/1⅔ cups boiling water and simmer for 30–40 minutes until tender. Stir in the fish and parsley and serve.

⬤ 🏺 ▽ ⭐ ✪ ⬆ 🔺 🔻 🔻

psyllium

NUTRIENTS
Calcium, magnesium, phosphorus, potassium, zinc; fibre

A powerful laxative, for centuries psyllium has been used in India for promoting digestive health.

As an alternative to the husks drink, you can buy psyllium in capsules from health-food shops.

Psyllium comes from the *Plantago ovata* plant and it is the ground husk of the seed that is used. It is excellent for cleansing the intestines, fighting bacterial and fungal infections. Scatter a tablespoon over soups and salads or, for persistent constipation or during a detox, use it as a daily drink. When taking psyllium, particularly as a constipation remedy, increase your water intake to eight large glasses a day.

PSYLLIUM HUSKS DRINK

**1 heaped tbsp psyllium
large glass of water**

Stir the psyllium into the water and drink immediately (to avoid the drink solidifying). Drink another glass of water.

quinoa

A perfect vegetable protein and slow-release energy food, this South American seed is becoming widely available and a must for dieters.

This deliciously nutty-tasting, gluten-free grain is very easy to digest and suitable for those with wheat intolerance or coeliac disease. Packed with vegetable protein, quinoa provides more calcium than milk and contains all eight amino acids. It also contains lysine which fights viral infections. The slow-release carbs regulate blood sugar, mood swings and cravings.

NUTRIENTS

Vitamins B3, B5, B6, folic acid; calcium, iron, magnesium, manganese, phosphorus, potassium, zinc; fibre; lysine; protein

VEGETABLE QUINOA

225g/8oz/1 cup quinoa
2 tsp vegetable bouillon
2 tbsp olive oil
2 onions, finely chopped
2 cloves garlic, crushed
2 green peppers, deseeded
  and diced
225g/8oz courgettes, sliced
225g/8oz tomatoes, chopped

Put the quinoa and bouillon in a pan with 300ml/10½fl oz/1¼ cups water, bring to the boil and simmer for 15 minutes. Heat the oil in another pan and fry the onions, peppers and garlic for 2 minutes. Add the remaining vegetables and cook for 2 minutes. Mix well with the quinoa and season to taste.

058

barley

As one of the diet-friendly complex carbs, barley is a top slow-release energy food that staves off hunger pangs and food cravings.

Barley is a mild laxative that is very soothing and stabilizing for the digestive tract. It is filling and warming and is particularly good in winter soups when you want to keep energy levels up without gaining weight. Sometimes called pearl barley, it should be soaked overnight in cold water before use.

NUTRIENTS

Vitamins B1, B2, B3, B5, B6, B9, B12, E, folic acid; calcium, iron, magnesium, manganese, phosphorus, zinc; fibre; protein

BARLEY AND BEAN BROTH

225g/8oz/1 cup dried beans (aduki, black-eye, kidney)
225g/8oz/1 cup pearl barley
2 large onions, chopped
4 carrots, chopped
4 sticks celery, chopped
175g/6oz spinach
4 tbsp tomato purée
2 tbsp miso
1 tsp sage
1 tbsp ground cumin
4 tbsp low-fat bio yogurt

Soak the beans and barley overnight. Next day, bring to the boil in 1.2 litres/2 pints/5 cups water with the next eight ingredients. Simmer for 45 minutes and serve with yogurt.

wholewheat pasta

This slow-release carb can form a nutritious part of your diet plan – fantastic news for pasta lovers.

Pasta is often avoided by dieters, but it is usually the sauce that is the problem. Choose wholewheat pasta (wheat-free varieties are also available) which contains more nutrients than white pasta and, as a less refined product, is harder to break down and store as fat. As it is high in fibre, the absorption of sugar is inhibited, too. And it's more filling than white, so you'll eat less.

NUTRIENTS
Vitamins B3, B5, B6, folic acid; calcium, iron, magnesium, manganese, phosphorus, potassium, zinc; fibre; protein

PASTA WITH THREE HERB SAUCE

300g/10½oz/1½ cups wholewheat pasta
1 tbsp olive oil
1 clove garlic, chopped
2 handfuls of chopped basil, parsley and tarragon leaves
2 tbsp vegetable bouillon
salt and ground black pepper

Boil the pasta in lightly salted water until al dente. Meanwhile, put the oil, garlic, herbs, bouillon and seasoning into a food processor and blend to make a smooth sauce. Drain the pasta and heap into a serving bowl. Pour over the herb sauce and serve.

090

lentil

NUTRIENTS

Vitamins B3, B5, B6, B9, folic acid; calcium, iron, magnesium, manganese, potassium, phosphorus, selenium, zinc; fibre; protein

LENTIL FACTS

• Lentils are anti-inflammatory and are especially helpful for rheumatoid arthritis.

• There is increasing evidence to suggest that lentils lower the risk of breast cancer and protect against fibroids (benign tumours in the uterus, most common in childless, pre-menopausal women over the age of 35).

• Lentils relieve menopausal symptoms, such as hot flushes and night sweats, and are often recommended by naturopaths as an alternative to HRT (hormone replacement therapy).

Bursting with protein and B vitamins, lentils are one of the best foods for stabilizing blood sugar and boosting energy levels.

Rich in minerals and fibre, lentils are excellent intestinal cleansers, increasing the amount of friendly bacteria in the gut that aid digestion. They are a staple of detoxifying diets and they also cleanse the blood and lower the levels of harmful LDL cholesterol. Because lentils contain a number of B vitamins, they have a stabilizing effect on blood pressure.

LENTIL AND CELERY SOUP

1 tbsp olive oil
1 onion, chopped
2 cloves garlic, crushed
225g/8oz/1 cup lentils
1 tbsp vegetable bouillon
1 head celery, chopped
juice of 1 lemon
salt and ground black pepper

Heat the olive oil in a saucepan and gently fry the onion and garlic for 2 minutes, then add 1.2 litres/2 pints/5 cups water, the lentils and bouillon. Bring to the boil and add the celery. Simmer, covered, for 20 minutes, stirring occasionally and checking water level. Add the lemon juice and season with black pepper and a little salt if necessary. Keep in the refrigerator and use within 2 days, or freeze.

Lentils are also a fantastic source of protein and iron – important for energy production and metabolism, making them an ideal food for vegetarians or those wishing to reduce animal fats in their diet. Their slow-release natural sugars make them a good form of complex carbohydrate, providing dieters with steady, slow-burning energy and preventing yo-yoing blood sugars and moods.

Lentils contain phytoestrogens which help stabilize erratic periods and PMS.

chickpea

High in fibre, chickpeas are fantastic for helping to maintain a healthy digestive system.

NUTRIENTS
Vitamins B1, B2, B3, B5, E, folic acid; calcium, iron, magnesium, manganese, phosphorus, potassium, zinc; fibre; protein

An excellent slow-release energy food, chickpeas are packed with nutrients, too. They are particularly rich in the antioxidant vitamin E, which helps to protect your body from infection while you diet. You can use them in soups and stews but hummus – the Greek dip made from chickpeas – is the dieter's tastiest friend. It's nutritious, versatile and can be a delicious salad dressing, healthy snack or light lunch. Spread it on oatcakes or use it as a dip with vegetable crudités, such as carrots, celery, cucumber, courgette and peppers.

HUMMUS

225g/8oz/1½ cups chickpeas
4 tbsp tahini
4 cloves garlic, chopped
juice of 2 lemons
2 tbsp olive oil
2 tsp ground cumin
4 tbsp fresh flat-leaf parsley

Soak the chickpeas overnight. Next day, drain, place in a pan and cover with water. Bring to the boil and simmer for 2 hours until soft. Drain, reserving 125ml/4fl oz/½ cup of the liquid. Put the chickpeas and remaining ingredients (including the reserved liquid) in a food processor and blend until creamy. Season with black pepper.

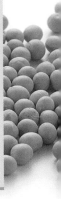

soya

The most nutritious of all beans, soya contains essential omega-3s and amino acids, as well as phytoestrogens, protein, minerals and vitamins.

Soya is one of the most versatile foods, available as beans for cooking, as a flour, as milk, miso, yogurt, tofu and soya sauce. Rich in fibre, it helps prevent or ease constipation. Its slow-release energy safeguards blood sugar balance and keeps hunger pangs and cravings at bay. Owing to its high levels of phytoestrogens (plant chemicals that mimic the hormone oestrogen), soya helps protect against hormone-based cancers such as breast, cervical, ovarian and prostate cancer.

NUTRIENTS
Vitamins B2, B6, C, E, folic acid; calcium, iron, magnesium, manganese, phosphorus, zinc; fibre; omega-3 fatty acids; phytoestrogens; protein

SHOYU DRESSING

Shoyu is a naturally fermented sauce made from soya beans that doesn't contain the sugar and additives often found in ordinary soya sauce. It has a stronger flavour, too.

185ml/6fl oz/¾ cup olive oil
2 tbsp shoyu
juice of 1 lemon
2 cloves garlic, crushed
ground black pepper

Place all the ingredients in a screwtop jar and shake well. This makes a substantial amount of dressing but it will keep in the refrigerator for up to 2 weeks.

063

sprouted seeds

Easy and quick to grow, sprouted seeds provide huge nutritional benefits and add low-calorie, healthy flavour to a wide variety of dishes.

SPROUTING SEEDS

seeds of your choice
gardeners' nylon mesh
gardeners' seed trays
gardeners' water spray

Place a couple of handfuls of seeds in a bowl, cover with water and leave overnight. Next day, drain and rinse. Place the seeds on top of the nylon mesh in a seed tray. Leave to sprout in a warm, dark place, spraying twice a day with water, stirring gently. When they have started to sprout, place them in the sun. Rinse and keep in the refrigerator to use in salads and other dishes.

When you sprout a seed, its vitamin content can increase by up to 2,000 percent within just a few days. Sprouted seeds are also very easily digested and absorbed by the body and are a good substitute for high-calorie dressing on salads. Buy seeds such as sesame and sunflower seeds, mung, aduki and soya beans, alfalfa, chickpeas and lentils, and add them to salads, soups and stir-fries.

alfalfa

Alfalfa can be sprinkled on to any salad or added to any sandwich to boost your mineral intake – at virtually no calorie cost.

Alfalfa is one of the few sprouted seeds that is readily available in supermarkets. You can add it to all kinds of sandwiches as well as salads for a deliciously mild flavour and extra texture. Alfalfa will also significantly boost zinc intake, particularly when combined with chicory, to improve both liver and hormone function as well as promoting cellular growth and renewal.

NUTRIENTS
Calcium, magnesium, manganese, potassium, sodium, zinc

ALFALFA SALAD

**225g/8oz mixed salad leaves
(such as lettuce, watercress
and spinach)
4 large tomatoes
115g/4oz/2 cups alfalfa sprouts
1 tsp white wine vinegar
2 tsp olive oil
1 spring onion, chopped
1 clove garlic, crushed
salt and ground black pepper,
to taste**

Wash the salad leaves, cut the tomatoes into wedges and mix with the alfalfa sprouts in a large bowl. For the dressing, mix together the remaining ingredients and pour over the salad just before serving.

nuts

NUTRIENTS
Vitamins B2, B3, C, E, folic acid; calcium, iron, magnesium, phosphorous, potassium, selenium, zinc; fibre; protein

---

RASPBERRY AND HAZELNUT CRUNCH

115g/4oz/1 cup hazelnuts, chopped and roasted
2 tbsp honey
115g/4oz/1¼ cups wholemeal breadcrumbs, toasted
280g/10oz/2½ cups raspberries
4 tbsp low-fat bio yogurt

Stir the hazelnuts and honey into the breadcrumbs. Layer with the raspberries in bowls and serve with the yogurt.

The many health-giving properties found in nuts make them an ideal occasional treat.

Nuts are an excellent form of protein and fibre, particularly important for vegetarians. Used in their raw form (unsalted and unprocessed), they are a rich source of antioxidant vitamins and minerals. Nuts are high in fat but it is "good" monounsaturated fat, which contributes to lowering "bad" LDL cholesterol when eaten in moderation. Cashews, walnuts, hazelnuts and almonds are among the most nutritious nuts: between them they contain a range of B vitamins, which metabolize food into energy.

pine nuts

Lower in total fat than most other nuts and high in protein and essential fats, pine nuts are a delicious replacement for those wanting to avoid animal proteins.

While most fats should be avoided by those wanting to lose weight or eat healthily, it is important to include certain fats in your diet. Pine nuts are a rich source of beneficial polyunsaturated fats, which actually increase the body's capacity to burn fat as well as helping to maintain low cholesterol and decrease the stickiness of the blood.

NUTRIENTS
Vitamins B1, B2, B3, E; calcium, iron, magnesium, manganese, zinc; protein

WATERCRESS AND PINE NUT SALAD

85g/3oz/½ cup pine nuts
175g/6oz watercress
1 avocado, peeled, stoned
    and chopped
4 tomatoes, chopped
2 tbsp olive oil
1 tsp white wine vinegar
1 tsp mustard
salt and ground black pepper

Lightly toast the pine nuts in a dry frying pan, turning continuously. Put the watercress, avocado and tomatoes in a bowl and scatter the toasted nuts on top. Make a dressing from the remaining ingredients, season to taste, pour over the salad and serve.

✳seeds

Together, sunflower, sesame and pumpkin seeds make a tasty, nutritious trio – try to use some every day in a wide variety of dishes.

All three of these seeds are beneficial for intestinal health, cleansing the digestive system and preventing constipation, while pectin, the soluble fibre found in sunflower seeds, is a particularly powerful detoxifier. Sesame seeds inhibit cholesterol absorption and their high levels of zinc and selenium are potent antioxidant cleansers.

Valuable sources of protein, these little seeds are rich in the essential omega-3 fatty acids, while sesame and sunflower seeds also contain the essential omega-6 fatty acids. Both of

NUTRIENTS

Vitamins A, B, D, E, K; calcium, iron, magnesium, manganese, phosphorus, zinc; omega-3 and omega-6 fatty acids; pectin; protein

SEED FACTS

• Sunflower seeds strengthen the eyesight and reduce the risk of cataracts.
• Sesame seeds strengthen the heart as well as the immune and nervous systems.
• Pumpkin seeds help in wound healing and are traditionally associated with prostate health and the prevention or reduction of bladder stones.
• Lightly toasting sunflower and sesame seeds in a dry frying pan will enhance their delicious, nutty flavour. However, pumpkin seeds should not be heated, as this will destroy some of their nutrients.
• Scatter a tablespoon of mixed seeds over soups and salads for added flavour and nutrients.

BREAKFAST SEEDY YOGURT

4 tbsp mixed sunflower, sesame and pumpkin seeds
400ml/14fl oz/1⅔ cups low-fat bio yogurt
1 tsp honey (optional)

Lightly toast the sunflower and sesame seeds in a dry frying pan. Remove from the heat and mix in the pumpkin seeds. Add to the yogurt and mix with honey for sweetness, if desired. You can add any fresh chopped fruit for variety – a perfect breakfast.

these groups of fatty acids must be provided by your diet as your body cannot manufacture them by itself and they are vital to health. They are necessary for the regeneration of healthy cells and protect against blood clotting and the risk of heart disease. They also nourish the skin, improve the symptoms of rheumatoid arthritis and may give protection against certain forms of cancer.

Seeds contain antioxidant zinc, which has powerful skin-boosting properties.

890

salmon

Deliciously tasty and textured, salmon is full of omega-3 fatty acids and one of the healthiest forms of protein – a first-rate fish for dieters.

The essential fatty acids found in salmon are not the fats dieters want to avoid but, as their name implies, fats that are essential for good health. These fats cannot be made within the body. They have a range of benefits, including strengthening cardiovascular health, controlling cholesterol levels, improving digestion and increasing the body's capacity to burn fat.

SALMON FISH CAKES

115g/4oz potatoes, quartered
115g/4oz sweet potatoes, quartered
280g/10oz salmon fillet, skinned
1 tbsp flour
2 tbsp olive oil

Boil the potatoes until just cooked. Meanwhile, chop the salmon into small pieces. In a bowl, mash the potatoes and combine with the salmon, then season. With floured hands, divide the mixture into four and form each into a "cake". Heat the oil in a frying pan and cook the fishcakes for 3 minutes on each side.

mackerel

Loaded with antioxidant selenium and vitamin E, mackerel is also an excellent source of protein.

Bursting with essential fatty acids, this oily fish is wonderfully hydrating for dry skin. Mackerel is also one of the few food sources of vitamin D (usually manufactured in the body from sunlight), which is essential for good bone development. The vitamin E and selenium contained in mackerel work well with its essential fatty acids to protect the heart. Eat mackerel with salad or leafy green vegetables for maximum benefits.

NUTRIENTS
Vitamins B3, B6, B12, D, E; calcium, iodine, potassium, selenium; omega-3 fatty acids; protein

SMOKED MACKEREL PÂTÉ

2 large smoked mackerel
85g/3oz low-fat bio yogurt
85g/3oz low-fat cottage cheese
1 tsp horseradish sauce
1 tbsp lemon juice
ground black pepper, to taste

Put all of the ingredients in a food processor and mix. Transfer to a bowl and chill in the refrigerator for 3 hours.

sardine

NUTRIENTS
Vitamins B3, B6, D, E; calcium, iodine, selenium; omega-3 fatty acids; protein

GRILLED SARDINES

2 tsp olive oil
1 tbsp dried oregano
juice of 2 lemons
ground black pepper
8 fresh sardines

With a fork, mix together the first four ingredients. Spread over the sardines and marinate for 1 hour. Grill or barbecue for 2 minutes on each side.

Super-quick to prepare, sardines are packed with healthy protein and omega-3s.

For added calcium, mash the soft bones that you find in canned sardines and eat them, too.

Fresh sardines are becoming more widely available and make a fantastic diet food. Canned sardines are wonderfully convenient and a good choice, too, providing you avoid ones that are canned in oil – which raises the calories and fats dramatically. The essential fatty acids and selenium found in sardines work together to give a double dose of heart health.

cod

Low in calories, fresh cod is an extremely tasty and versatile white fish.

Cod is often deep-fried in batter or covered in breadcrumbs. Dieters should avoid both of these and look instead for the fresh white fish that can be cooked in a variety of ways that won't load on the calories, such as baking or steaming. Cod is a particularly good source of the mineral magnesium, which regulates the adrenal glands and helps control metabolism. It also has very low salt levels compared with most other fish.

NUTRIENTS
Magnesium; protein

FISH AND FENNEL SOUP

400g/14oz cod
2 tbsp wholemeal flour
2 tsp tamari
1 tbsp olive oil
juice 1 lemon
225g/8oz turnips, chopped
1.2 litres/2 pints/5 cups water
2 tbsp vegetable bouillon
1 onion, chopped
1 large or 2 small fennel
   bulbs, chopped
1 tsp cayenne pepper

Bone and skin the cod. Make a smooth paste of the flour, tamari, oil, lemon juice and a little water, as needed. Put the turnips, water and bouillon in a pan and bring to the boil. Add the onion, fennel and cayenne and stir in the paste. Simmer for 10 minutes. Add the fish and cook for 10 minutes more.

tuna

NUTRIENTS

Vitamins B3, B6, B12, D, E, biotin; iodine, calcium, selenium; omega-3 fatty acids; protein; tryptophan

TUNA FACTS

• Fresh tuna is particularly nutritious – always look for firm flesh and a clear eye. It can be eaten raw or cooked (it needs little cooking time).

• Canned tuna loses its omega-3 fatty acids in the canning process but it is still a good diet food – just make sure it has no added oil, salt or other undesirable additives.

• The essential fatty acids in fresh tuna reduce the symptoms of PMS, especially mood swings and irritability – further aided by tryptophan, a calming amino acid.

• The biotin and vitamin B3 found in fresh tuna are anti-inflammatory, helping to reduce the painful symptoms of rheumatoid arthritis.

Best cooked by grilling or on a griddle, fresh tuna is a wonderful fish for dieters – it is a great detoxifier and immunity-booster.

Tuna contains selenium, an important antioxidant mineral that detoxifies the body by attacking free radicals and removing heavy metals, such as mercury, from the system, helping protect against cancer. Selenium also strengthens the immune system generally, raising the white blood cell count and improving resistance to infection – particularly crucial while you lose weight. Tuna is also a superb source of essential fatty acids, important for burning excess fat, balancing blood sugar

TUNA TERIYAKI

4 tbsp shoyu
1 tbsp runny honey
2 cloves garlic, crushed
1 tbsp lemon juice
2 tbsp olive oil
ground black pepper
4 tuna steaks

Make a marinade by mixing the first six ingredients. Coat the tuna in some marinade and leave to marinate for 3 hours. Grill the tuna for 3 minutes on each side, adding a little marinade to stop the fish drying out. Serve with any remaining marinade, warmed through.

levels and banishing hunger pangs, as well as reducing the risk of stroke and lowering both cholesterol and high blood pressure, thus protecting the heart. High in healthy protein, tuna helps to maintain lean muscle mass which also encourages the fat-burning process. Tuna improves dry skin and is thought to be a key food in the reduction of cellulite.

Tuna, like all fish, contains sodium – so no added salt is needed.

oyster

NUTRIENTS
Vitamins A, B3, B12, C, D, E; calcium, iron, magnesium, selenium, zinc; omega-3 fatty acids; protein

ONION AND OYSTER SOUP

1 tbsp olive oil
450g/1lb onions, chopped
1 small can oysters
1 tbsp vegetable bouillon
juice of 1 lemon
handful of fresh herbs (such as coriander or parsley)
570ml/1 pint/2½ cups water

Heat the olive oil in a saucepan and sauté the onions, with a little water. Add the remaining ingredients and bring to the boil. Simmer for 10 minutes, season to taste and serve.

Low in calories and fat, this mouthwatering shellfish is also the highest possible source of the essential, immune-boosting mineral zinc.

Famed as aphrodisiacs, oysters contain exceptional amounts of zinc which helps the liver to detoxify and supports healthy reproductive function, as well as boosting immunity and resistance to infection. They are a superb source of several other important minerals, including magnesium and selenium. Magnesium regulates metabolic rate and selenium is a potent antioxidant, which also improves the function of the liver.

prawn

High in nutrients and low in fat, prawns are a wonderfully versatile and delicious diet food.

Containing very little fat and virtually no saturated fat, prawns provide good levels of zinc and selenium. These minerals strengthen the immune system and increase resistance to infection. They also improve liver function. As the waste disposal unit of the body, the liver needs to be working at optimum level to eliminate toxins and waste most efficiently. It also plays a part in metabolizing fat. Prawns are high in salt, so wash before use and never add any extra salt to prawn dishes.

NUTRIENTS
Vitamins B3, B12; calcium, iodine, magnesium, phosphorus, potassium, selenium, zinc; fibre; protein

The zinc found in prawns is beneficial for women taking oral contraceptives.

KING PRAWN SALAD

8 cooked king-size prawns, peeled
3 handfuls of mixed salad leaves and herbs
1 tsp olive oil
1 tbsp lemon juice

In a bowl, mix the prawns with the leaves and herbs. Drizzle over the oil and lemon juice and sprinkle with black pepper.

⬤ ◉ ◉ ⬤ ▼ ★ ✪ ✖ ✖ ✖

chicken

The most popular source of animal protein, chicken can make a healthy slimming option.

Chicken can be a nutritious part of your diet plan, but deep-fried "Southern-style" is to be avoided at all costs, and so is the skin of roast chicken and the creamy sauces that are often found in dishes such as coronation chicken – all guaranteed to pile on the pounds. Instead, buy skinless chicken breasts or remove the skin when you cook it yourself. Whenever possible, choose organic chicken for optimum health and flavour.

White chicken meat contains less fat and fewer calories than the darker meat.

NUTRIENTS

Vitamins A, B3, B6, K; magnesium, potassium, selenium; protein

CHICKEN CURRY

2 tbsp olive oil
4 skinless chicken breasts,
    cut into strips
4 cloves garlic, crushed
4 onions, chopped
2 tsp ground coriander
2 tsp ground turmeric
1 red chilli pepper
1 tbsp vegetable bouillon
4 tbsp low-fat bio yogurt

Heat the oil in a large saucepan and fry the chicken for 2 minutes. Set aside. Add the garlic, onions and spices to the pan and fry until the onion is soft. Return the chicken to the pan, pour in 400ml/14fl oz/1⅔ cups boiling water and add the bouillon. Simmer for 20 minutes. Top with yogurt and serve with brown basmati rice.

turkey

Full of vitamins and minerals, turkey is another excellent source of low-fat protein for dieters.

A whole roast turkey is often the centre of a big family party, but smaller portions are increasingly available and can be cooked in a healthy, low-fat way. As with chicken, avoid the skin and steer clear of rich sauces. Turkey is a good source of the immunity-boosting minerals zinc and selenium, as well as B vitamins, which aid metabolism. The darker meat found on the leg has more iron and zinc than the white breast meat.

NUTRIENTS
Vitamins B3, B6, B12; iron, selenium, zinc; protein

TURKEY AND ORANGE CASEROLE

4 small skinless turkey breast steaks or legs
2 onions, finely chopped
2 sticks celery, finely chopped
1 tbsp fresh herbs
grated rind and juice of 2 oranges
1 tbsp vegetable bouillon
watercress, to garnish

Place the turkey, onions and celery in a casserole. Add the herbs, orange rind and juice and season to taste. Mix the vegetable bouillon with 150ml/5fl oz/⅔ cup boiling water and pour over the turkey. Cover and cook in a preheated oven at 180°C/350°F/Gas Mark 4 for 1 hour. Garnish with watercress and serve.

liver

A superbly rich source of iron, liver helps maintain good blood health and build muscle.

The iron in liver also helps metabolize protein. This process works most efficiently when iron and protein are absorbed from an animal source (such as liver), which combines the two nutrients. Liver contains much more selenium than most other meat – a cancer-fighting antioxidant that helps to detoxify the human liver. Although liver is high in cholesterol, it is very low in saturated fat that can lead to weight gain and health risks.

NUTRIENTS
Vitamins A, B3, B6, biotin, folic acid; iron, selenium; protein

PEPPERED CALF'S LIVER

4 pieces calf's liver
1 tsp olive oil
2 tbsp crushed black pepper
pinch of salt
2 tbsp chopped fresh herbs

Slice the liver thinly, brush with olive oil and press in the black pepper, then sprinkle with salt. Griddle for 2 minutes on each side and scatter with herbs. Serve on top of a mixed green salad or with potato and celeriac mash (see page 39).

partridge

This small game bird is rich in protein and other nutrients but low in saturated fat and cholesterol.

Like all game, partridges are free to move around and so they acquire fewer harmful fats than their farmed equivalents. They are an excellent source of all the essential B vitamins, important for a wide range of functions, including digestion and food metabolism. Always buy game from a reputable butcher. Young birds should be roasted slowly, while older ones are better braised or casseroled.

NUTRIENTS
Vitamins B1, B2, B3, B5, B6, B12; iron, selenium, zinc; protein

BRAISED PARTRIDGE

2 small partridges, cut into portions
6 tbsp olive oil
2 cloves garlic, crushed
4 sprigs thyme
4 bay leaves
3 sticks celery, chopped
2 tbsp vegetable bouillon
2 onions, chopped

Put the partridges in a bowl with a marinade made from the other ingredients (except for the onions and 1 tbsp oil) and season to taste. Leave to marinate overnight. Next day, heat the 1 tbsp oil in a frying pan and brown the partridges. Set aside. Fry the onions in the same pan. Add the remaining marinade and the partridges and cook for 30 minutes.

venison

NUTRIENTS
Vitamins B1, B2, B3, B5, B6, B12;
iron, zinc; protein

VENISON FACTS
• Venison has a high iron content
which is needed for healthy blood.
A lack of iron can cause anaemia,
particularly among pregnant
women or those who have
heavy periods.
• When roasting a haunch of
venison, use a covered roasting tin
as venison lacks the covering of fat
that bastes other joints naturally.
Do not leave to stand before
serving, but carve into very thin
slices immediately after it is cooked
and serve on very hot plates.
• Because venison steaks are so
lean, they require very little
cooking. If in doubt, cook for less
time rather than more.

A fantastically lean and nutritious form of protein,
venison is very low in fat and rich in flavour, and
so doesn't need rich, fat-laden sauces.

One of the healthiest forms of protein, venison comes from a
wide variety of free-range deer, and so it is not usually
subjected to the barrage of antibiotics, growth supplements
and dubious farming practices suffered by many farm animals.
And, because it is free to move around, it acquires less fat than
farmed animals, too.

While an excessive intake of animal protein is not good for
health, eating game once or twice a week can be very

SESAME VENISON STEAKS

4 lean venison steaks
2 cloves garlic, crushed
1 tbsp grated fresh root ginger
4 tbsp shoyu
2 tbsp olive oil
2 tbsp sesame seeds, toasted
200g/7oz noodles, cooked

Place the venison in a bowl
and marinate in the mixed garlic,
ginger, shoyu and oil for 2 hours.
Cook the venison on a griddle or
in a frying pan for 2 minutes on
each side, then cut into thick
slices. To serve, toss the sesame
seeds with the cooked noodles
and top with the venison.

beneficial. Like all game, venison is extremely nutrient-rich, containing all the essential amino acids needed to make new tissues, blood, hormones and enzymes, which the body uses to repair and rebuild cells and strengthen the immune system, keeping you in top health as you diet.

Venison contains all the essential B vitamins, vital for the processing of food into energy: between them they play a crucial role in the metabolism of sugars, proteins and carbohydrates, and strengthen the digestive system, too.

The term venison also applies to the meats of moose, elk, caribou and antelope.

080

duck

NUTRIENTS
Vitamin B2; iron, zinc; protein

Duck is a highly nutritious and delicious form of protein. The secret of including it in your weight-loss diet is to remove all of the fat and skin.

You can enjoy duck in moderation as part of your diet, providing you use careful cooking methods. If you roast a duck, do so on a trivet so that the fat drains into the tray and then remove all the skin before serving. Although duck is high in cholesterol, it is low in saturated fat – lower than chicken, in fact, when all the skin is removed. Ducks' amino acids help vitamins and minerals to perform their functions effectively and the body to repair cells and strengthen the immune system.

DUCK BREAST SALAD

2 tbsp sesame oil
1 tbsp white wine vinegar
4 handfuls of mixed salad leaves
2 duck breasts, all fat removed
1 tsp olive oil
55g/2oz/⅓ cup pine nuts

In a jug, mix the sesame oil and white wine vinegar and pour over the salad leaves. Arrange the salad on four plates. Slice the duck breasts and brush with olive oil, then cook on a griddle or in a frying pan for 2 minutes on each side. Add the pine nuts and cook for a further 2 minutes. Place the duck and pine nuts on the salad and serve.

081

egg

An excellent low-fat source of protein, eggs are a good slow-release energy food, stabilizing blood sugar levels and keeping hunger pangs at bay.

NUTRIENTS
Vitamins A, B3, B6, E; calcium, iron, manganese, zinc; protein

Low in saturated fats and high in protein, eggs are also superb immunity builders and even improve brain (particularly memory) function. They also have a high zinc content which is beneficial for tissue repair and healing, as well as liver function. The vitamin E contained in eggs is a powerful antioxidant, which thins the blood and fights harmful free radicals. Eating too many eggs can cause constipation, and they are also high in cholesterol, so include them in your diet in moderation.

SMOKED SALMON WITH SCRAMBLED EGGS

6 medium free-range eggs
salt and ground black pepper
1 tsp olive oil
85g/3oz smoked salmon
4 tbsp dill or chives
lemon wedges, to garnish

Beat the eggs with the salt and pepper and heat in a pan with the oil, stirring all the time until just cooked. Pile on plates with the smoked salmon, sprinkle over the herbs and garnish with lemon wedges and more black pepper.

tofu

NUTRIENTS
Vitamins A, K; boron, calcium, iron, magnesium, phosphorus, potassium, selenium; fibre; omega-3 fatty acids; phytoestrogens; protein

---

PEPPERY TOFU DIP

225g/8oz-packet silken tofu
2 tbsp lemon juice
1 tbsp olive oil
1 clove garlic, crushed
salt and ground black pepper

Put all the ingredients in a food processor and blend until smooth. Serve with vegetable crudités.

Made from nutrient-rich soya beans, tofu is one of the best vegetarian forms of protein for dieters.

A versatile, low-fat food, tofu is available in both firm and soft forms and can be used in many vegetarian recipes. As miso it makes an ideal basis for soups and stocks. Like all soya products, it is rich in calcium and protein and has potent cancer-fighting properties. It is free from saturated fat and, unlike many animal proteins, helps reduce high blood pressure and cholesterol levels. Tofu is also a good source of fibre and slow-release energy, staving off food cravings.

low-fat cheese

From dieters' tasty standbys, such as cottage cheese, to low-fat versions of favourites, such as Cheddar, cheese can be a creamy treat for dieters.

Renowned low-fat cheeses such as cottage cheese make a healthy snack – just don't eat a whole pot at a sitting. Instead, use as a dip with celery, cucumber and carrot crudités. Rightly avoided by dieters, full-fat cheeses are high in saturated fat and calories and have long been linked to raised cholesterol levels. In many supermarkets and delicatessens there are now low-fat versions of popular cheeses, which can be enjoyed in moderation as a treat or used in cooking for added flavour.

NUTRIENTS
Vitamins B2, B12; calcium, magnesium, phosphorus, potassium; protein

CHEESE AND WALNUT LOAF

225g/8oz cottage or curd cheese
55g/2oz/¼ cup walnuts, ground
2 tsp wholegrain mustard
115g/4oz/1¼ cups wholemeal breadcrumbs
2 medium free-range eggs, beaten

Mix the ingredients and put in a lightly oiled loaf tin. Bake in a preheated oven at 180°C/350°F/ Gas Mark 4 for 30 minutes.

ricotta cheese

Delicious and versatile, ricotta is made from whey and is a very low-fat cheese.

Ricotta can be made from the separated whey of cow's or sheep's milk – choose the latter if you think you may have an intolerance to cow's milk. It is very low in fat but has a soft, creamy texture. Ricotta's vitamin B5 supports the adrenal glands, which regulate the body's response to stress and help control the metabolism of fats, proteins and carbohydrates. For the best results, eat with foods rich in magnesium (almonds, green leafy vegetables) and vitamin C.

PEPPERS WITH RICOTTA

2 large red peppers
1 onion, finely chopped
225g/8oz tomatoes, chopped
2 tsp chopped fresh basil
115g/4oz ricotta cheese
4 tbsp low-fat bio yogurt

Grill the peppers until the skin blackens. Peel off the skin and slice the flesh into rings. Put the onion and tomatoes in a casserole and sprinkle with the basil and some black pepper. Add the pepper rings and spoon in a mixture of ricotta and yogurt. Bake in a preheated oven at 180°C/350°F/Gas Mark 4 for 30 minutes.

fromage frais

A wonderful substitute for cream, fromage frais turns desserts into a tasty, guilt-free treat.

If you crave cream and ice cream, fromage frais is a delicious low-fat, sugar-free alternative. And is one of those dairy foods that dieters occasionally need to give them a lift. Buy the low-fat version – it's virtually fat-free and made from skimmed milk to keep calorie counts down and lower "bad" LDL cholesterol. It has a tangy, slightly nutty taste and the consistency of yogurt, though it can be made thicker by whipping. You can also use it in savoury dishes that call for cream.

NUTRIENTS
Calcium; protein

Fromage frais originated in France and literally means "fresh cheese".

STRAWBERRIES WITH FROMAGE FRAIS

225g/8oz/2 cups strawberries, hulled and washed
1 tsp honey
juice of 1 orange
4 tbsp low-fat fromage frais

Put the strawberries in a bowl. Mix the honey and orange juice into the fromage frais and spoon over the strawberries.

bio yogurt

NUTRIENTS
Vitamins B2, B12, D; calcium, magnesium, potassium; protein

YOGURT FACTS
• Fruit yogurts should be avoided as they have a high sugar content.
• When yogurts are heat-treated, they lose their natural "friendly" bacteria, so add yogurt when cooking is finished, to sauces, soups and stews, for a creamy flavour and texture.
• Yogurt's high calcium levels ensure strong bones and teeth. It is particularly beneficial for post-menopausal women who run the risk of losing bone density owing to osteoporosis.

A brilliant, low-fat source of protein, bio yogurt is a natural antibiotic that improves digestive health.

Buy low-fat bio (live) yogurt for minimum calories and maximum health benefits. Yogurt is produced by the action of friendly bacteria on the sugars in milk (lactose), turning them into lactic acid. We do this in our own bodies when we drink milk, but the resulting lactose is often the cause of a food intolerance to dairy products. However, bio yogurt contains friendly bacteria called *Lactobacillus acidophilus* that help break down lactose, and so most people find it much easier to digest. These friendly bacteria support the body's own "flora" (friendly bacteria in the gut), ensuring good intestinal function. This is particularly beneficial when flora levels are low – for example, if you are under stress or after a course of antibiotics.

FRUITY YOGURT

4 large peaches, pears or nectarines 115g/4oz low-fat bio yogurt	2 tbsp toasted almonds, finely chopped pinch of ground cinnamon 1 tbsp honey (optional)	Slice the fruit into a bowl and stir in the yogurt. Sprinkle with the nuts and cinnamon and stir. Serve for breakfast or as a snack.

Bio yogurt is also helpful for those suffering from yeast infections such as candida and helps prevent infections of the urinary tract. It is an excellent source of calcium and contains B vitamins and other immune-boosting minerals, helping the body to fight infection while you lose weight. Add low-fat bio yogurt to savoury dishes for a deliciously smooth, cooling flavour or serve with desserts as a low-fat alternative to cream.

In folk medicine, yogurt is associated with good health and long life.

087

Low-fat milk

NUTRIENTS
Vitamins B2, B12; calcium; protein

Low-fat milk is a fabulous fat-burner.

Low-fat dairy foods of all kinds can increase fat-burning. This may be due to their calcium content that encourages the release of fat from the fat cells and simultaneously reduces fat absorption. Perhaps even more interesting is that the fat is generally lost predominantly in the abdominal area. Nevertheless, you should try to moderate your dairy intake – drink (decaffeinated) tea and coffee weaker than usual and you will need to add less milk.

Choose organic milk when possible – it contains many more nutrients.

PRUNE SMOOTHIE

115g/4oz soaked prunes
200ml/7fl oz/¾ cup low-fat or soya milk

Blend the prunes and milk in a food processor and serve for breakfast or as a snack.

green tea

A low-caffeine form of tea, green tea is a superb calorie burner and contains powerful antioxidants.

Research has shown that drinking five cups of green tea every day can raise the number of calories your body naturally burns off by as many as 80. This may be due to the catechins (antioxidants) in green tea that boost the metabolism and break down fat. Green tea also contains potent antioxidants called polyphenols, free-radical scavengers that can lower blood pressure, thus reducing the risk of heart disease and stroke. It is also believed that green tea may reduce the risk of lung, colon and stomach cancer.

NUTRIENTS
Polyphenols

PRUNE AND GREEN TEA MOUSSE

1 orange, sliced (rind left on)
1 lemon, sliced (rind left on)
4 cinnamon sticks
1 vanilla pod
pot of green tea (500ml/17fl oz/
  2 cups), steeped for 5 minutes
375g/13oz prunes, stoned
1 tbsp honey
4 tbsp low-fat bio yogurt

Put the orange and lemon slices into a saucepan with the cinnamon and vanilla. Cover with the tea, bring to the boil and simmer for 10 minutes. Add the prunes, remove from the heat and put in a bowl. Add the honey, remove the cinnamon, vanilla, lemon and orange and blend to a purée. Chill in the refrigerator for 2 hours. Serve with the yogurt.

herbal tea

Delicately flavoured and caffeine-free, herbal teas can make up part of your daily water intake.

MINT TEA

handful of mint leaves
boiling water

Wash and tear the leaves and place in a teapot. Pour over boiling water and leave to infuse for 5–10 minutes.

You can buy a range of herbal tea bags in supermarkets or simply use a handful of herbs infused in boiling water for at least five minutes. Herbal teas are superbly hydrating and the herbs themselves have many health benefits for dieters. For example, peppermint is good for digestion; chamomile improves sleep and is also good for digestive problems; ginger is a general stimulant, boosting circulation; and fennel prevents flatulence.

Add a ¼ teaspoon honey to your herbal tea if you need a sweetener.

water

Essential to life, water is crucial to the smooth functioning of the body – without it all bodily systems become sluggish and less efficient.

Our bodies are, or should be, made up of at least 75 percent water. But we lose water all the time through urination, every time we exhale and – a staggering 1 litre/1¾ pints/4 cups a day – through the skin. And we rarely drink enough to replenish it.

Some people don't drink enough water because they think any fluid will do. Nothing could be further from the truth. Popular drinks such as coffee, tea, cola (and other drinks containing caffeine) and alcohol actually dehydrate the body. While an occasional cup of tea or coffee or glass of wine is not going to harm you, the only liquid that is going to hydrate you is water itself – or herbal tea.

Water is essential for digestive and urinary health. Without enough water, peristalsis in the gut ceases to work properly, resulting in constipation and toxic build-up – bad news for dieters. It is equally crucial to kidney health, flushing away toxins, helping your body to metabolize stored fat.

If you suffer from water retention, you need to drink even more water to help the body release fluids. Drinking plenty of water also keeps skin looking supple and young, and improves concentration and respiratory health.

YOU NEED TO DRINK 2 LITRES OF WATER A DAY, AND MORE WHEN:
- the weather is very hot
- you work in a centrally heated or air-conditioned environment
- you exercise
- you travel by air

⬤ ⬤ 🍶 🔻 ✪ ✪ ⇔ 🔪 🔪 🔥

*juices

Cleansing, energizing and rejuvenating, fresh, raw juices are a truly unbeatable staple of weight-loss diets and detoxification.

NUTRIENTS

In carrot and apple juice: vitamin C, beta-carotene, folic acid; calcium, iron, magnesium, phosphorus, potassium

JUICE FACTS

• You must use a juicing machine – food processors and blenders don't work unless they have a special juicing attachment.

• Vary juices so you have a wide range of nutrients.

• When juicing, always try to opt for organic fruit and vegetables for maximum levels of nutrition and reduced chemical resides from fertilizers and pesticides.

• Whenever possible, scrub the surface of the fruit or vegetable rather than peeling as the nutrients often lie just beneath the skin.

• Dilute very sweet juices with water to prevent a sudden surge in blood sugar levels.

• Very fibrous fruits or vegetables, such as figs or avocados, should be avoided as they produce little or no juice.

You can buy cartons of juice, but for the real thing invest in a juicer and make your own – nothing beats homemade, fresh juices when it comes to taste and nutrition, and there are so many delicious combinations of raw ingredients that you'll never get bored. Not only are fruits and vegetables low in fat, but they are also packed with vital vitamins, minerals and enzymes, which your body can absorb at top speed in juice form. Plus, because juices are raw none of these vital nutrients have been destroyed by cooking.

You can juice just about any combination of fruit or vegetables, but don't mix the two, with the exception of apple and carrot. Many vegetables – particularly green ones such as broccoli or watercress – have a strong or bitter flavour and should be mixed with sweeter types such as carrot or beetroot.

A day of juice fasting is a great way to kick-start a weight-loss diet. It is an exceptionally cleansing and rejuvenating treatment, expelling long-standing toxins, improving skin tone and shrinking appetite. You should spend at least one day preparing by eating only raw food (fruit and vegetable salads) and low-fat bio yogurt and drinking three large freshly made juices. On the juice fast day, drink three or four large freshly made juices (at least two of which should be vegetable-based) and eight large glasses of water (you can substitute herbal tea for some of these). After the fast, repeat the preparation day for one or two days. Not only should you notice that you've lost a few pounds, but you may have less of an appetite and better skin, too.

APPLE AND CARROT JUICE

8 carrots, scrubbed
4 large apples, washed

Juice the carrots, then apples. Stir and serve immediately.

smoothies

Creamy and rich, smoothies are full of nutritional goodness, low in fat and easy to make.

NUTRIENTS
Vitamins B2, B12, D; calcium, magnesium, potassium; protein (from the yogurt), plus further nutrients depending on fruits used

A smoothie makes an excellent breakfast or mid-morning snack – simply put all of the ingredients into a food processor or blender and mix. And because they are made from yogurt mixed with blended whole fruits, not only are they a fantastic source of protein, vitamins and minerals, but they also contain all the fruits' fibre – important for stimulating digestion and combating water retention and bloating. Use low-fat bio yogurt, or soya yogurt for the most diet-friendly drink and add fruit according to taste and season. Banana, apricot, grape, mango and all berries work well.

Sprinkle toasted mixed seeds on top of your smoothie for a crunchy texture and added nutrition.

SUMMER BERRY SMOOTHIE

225g/8oz/1⅔ cups strawberries
225g/8oz/1⅔ cups raspberries
250ml/9fl oz/1 cup low-fat bio yogurt

Wash the berries, hulling the strawberries, and place in a food processor. Blend until smooth and serve.

olives and olive oil

Easily digested, olives and their oil stimulate bowel function, aiding detoxification.

Paradoxically for an oil, olive oil can help you lose weight because it contains essential fatty acids which enable unwanted, stored fat to be removed from the system. However, it should be used only in moderation as excessive consumption will have the opposite effect. Olives have a high vitamin E content, a powerful anti-ageing antioxidant that also strengthens the immune system to keep you healthy while you lose weight, as well as lowering high cholesterol levels and blood pressure, reducing the risk of heart disease.

NUTRIENTS
Vitamin E, beta-carotene; iron, calcium

GREEK SALAD

55g/2oz feta cheese, cubed
½ cucumber, diced
20 fresh black olives, stoned and chopped
2 tomatoes, diced
1 green pepper, deseeded and sliced into strips
1 onion, sliced into rings
3 tbsp olive oil
juice of 1 lemon
salt and ground black pepper

Put all the salad ingredients in a salad bowl and pour over the olive oil and lemon juice. Season to taste and serve.

honey

Twice as sweet as sugar, honey is a good choice for sweet-toothed dieters as a little goes a long way.

NUTRIENTS
Vitamin C; calcium, iron; fibre

HONEY AND GINGER ICE CREAM

thumb-sized piece of fresh root ginger, peeled and finely chopped
2 tbsp honey
500ml/17fl oz/2 cups low-fat bio yogurt

Put the ginger and honey in a small pan, add a little water and boil, stirring, for 10 minutes. Leave to cool. When cold, stir into the yogurt. Transfer to a freezer-proof container and freeze for 4 hours; remove, stir and return to the freezer for a further 4 hours. Serve with tropical fruit.

Most dieters avoid sugar in their bid to prevent weight gain. However, they may have more sweetness in their diet than they are aware of – sugar is in most processed foods, bread, fizzy drinks, canned vegetables and pulses (such as baked beans) and alcohol. Cut out processed foods, and you will automatically lower your intake of hidden sugars. You can then wean yourself off sugar altogether by switching to using moderate amounts of honey, which is also mildly laxative and good for digestion.

carob

A sweet, low-fat substitute for chocolate, carob has the added bonus of being caffeine-free.

Rich in minerals, including calcium, as well as a little protein, carob is actually good for you. It has a much lower fat content than chocolate and is actually sweeter than cocoa, but contains fewer calories. You can buy it as a powder for use in desserts and cakes – always try to buy raw rather than toasted carob. When you substitute carob for cocoa in recipes, use about half the quantity suggested. And, over time, try gradually to reduce your sweetness quota to keep your overall calorie count down.

NUTRIENTS
Vitamins A, B1, B2; calcium, iron, magnesium, phosphorus, potassium; protein; silicon

CAROB PEARS

honey
150ml/5fl oz/⅔ cup orange juice
1 vanilla pod
4 sweet, ripe pears, peeled (stalks left on)
25g/1oz carob powder

Dissolve the honey in the orange juice and a little water in a pan over a low heat. Add the vanilla pod, stand the pears in the mixture, cover and poach until tender. Transfer the pears to four individual glass dishes. Gradually add the carob to the honey and orange mixture, making a roux and finally a running consistency, stirring. Pour over the pears.

vegetable bouillon

NUTRIENTS

Vitamin C, beta-carotene; calcium, potassium

Quick and easy to use, vegetable bouillon powder is the handy diet alternative to stock cubes.

Vegetable bouillon powder can be a diet drink – just add 1 teaspoon to 1 cup boiling water.

Available in most supermarkets, vegetable bouillon powder has many benefits compared to conventional stock cubes. It is gluten-, yeast- and dairy-free and contains a range of tasty, health-boosting herbs and spices. Low-salt and vegan versions are available, too. Use in soups, dressings, sauces and all kinds of savoury dishes – you can sprinkle the powder straight into the recipe, without having to dissolve in water first.

CHILLED PEA SOUP

115g/4oz French beans, chopped
115g/4oz peas
2 tbsp vegetable bouillon
6 spring onions, chopped
2 tbsp chopped fresh parsley
2 tbsp chopped fresh mint
400ml/14fl oz/1⅔ cups low-fat bio yogurt

Drop the French beans and the peas into a saucepan of boiling water with the vegetable bouillon and simmer for 4–5 minutes. Drain and reserve the water for stock. In a bowl, mix the remaining ingredients. Add the vegetables and gradually stir in the stock. Chill for 2 hours and serve.

spices

Intensely flavoursome and fat free, spices are an essential item in every dieter's kitchen cupboard.

In the war against salt – which contributes to everything from water retention to high blood pressure, spices are an invaluable weapon. They are full of flavour and can add zing to any dish, from soups and stews to desserts, without adding fat. Try to buy organic spices and always look for the whole spice rather than powdered – this is especially true of nutmegs, cloves, cinnamon sticks, vanilla pods, saffron and root ginger.

NUTRIENTS
Vary between individual spices, but include: vitamins B1, B2, C; calcium, manganese, phosphorus, potassium; omega-3 and omega-6 fatty acids; volatile oils

GINGER AND LEMON DRINK

thumb-sized piece of fresh root ginger
1 lemon

Peel and roughly chop the ginger and chop the lemon. Put both in a teapot or a vacuum flask and cover with boiling water. Drink throughout the day, particularly as part of a detoxification.

098

⬤ ◯ 🥤 ▽ ✪ ✪ ⇔ 🥘 🔪 🔪

chilli

NUTRIENTS
Vitamins B3, B6, C, E, K,
beta-carotene, folic acid; calcium,
copper, iodine, iron, magnesium,
phosphorus, potassium, zinc; fibre;
glucosinolates

The Mayans used chillies as weapons in battle, throwing them at the enemy.

Hot and fiery, chillies are a great way of spicing up your food without adding harmful salt or fats, plus they are first-rate fat-burners.

Recent research has shown that chillies and chilli-based sauces, such as Tabasco, can increase your calorie burn by up to 8 percent for two hours after eating. This is because the capsaicin found in chilli peppers is a supernutrient that speeds up your metabolism and helps you to burn off more energy.

Red and green chillies come in many sizes, and some are far hotter than others. If you are not used to cooking with chillies, use them sparingly to start with. Chop them carefully and always wash your hands immediately afterwards – if a

---

CHILLI CON CARNE

200g/7oz/2 cups dried kidney
  beans, soaked overnight and
  drained
1 onion, diced
2 cloves garlic, crushed
2 tsp chilli flakes
1 carrot, diced

2 tsp olive oil
450g/1lb lean minced beef
400g/14oz can chopped tomatoes
4 tsp vegetable bouillon

Put the beans in a saucepan of
water and boil fast for 10 minutes,

then simmer, covered, for a
further 30 minutes. Sauté the
onion, garlic, chilli flakes and
carrot in the oil for 5 minutes.
Add the remaining ingredients
and cooked beans. Simmer for
15 minutes and season to taste.

chilli-stained finger touches your eye, you will regret it! Remember, too, that the seeds are particular firebrands. You can also use dried chilli flakes – again, use them sparingly; you can always add more. But if you do overdo it, you can calm down the heat with a dollop or two of plain low-fat bio yogurt.

Because they heat you up, chillies are good for fighting off colds and coughs and other respiratory infections.

CHILLI FACTS
- Eating chillies releases endorphins that lift your mood.
- Weight for weight chillies contain about twice as much vitamin C as citrus fruits.
- Capsaicin cream is used to lessen the sensation of pain in arthritis and other painful chronic conditions.

herbs

Fresh, aromatic herbs can lift any dish and have fantastic health-giving properties, too.

NUTRIENTS
Vary between individual herbs, but include: vitamin C, beta-carotene; calcium, iron, magnesium, sodium; volatile oils

Parsley is a potent cleanser, particularly of the blood and kidneys, and contains high levels of vitamin C to boost the immune system. Thyme reduces bloating and irritable bowel syndrome, and also contains thymol, an oil that helps to digest fatty foods. Rosemary boosts circulation and is a general tonic and detoxifier, especially for the heart and the digestive system. Sage acts on bloating and indigestion. Chives have similar benefits to onions (see page 38) and mint boosts digestion.

FRIED PARSLEY

2 tsp olive oil
2 large bunches parsley
2 tbsp pine nuts
4 tbsp toasted mixed seeds

In a frying pan, heat the oil and gently fry the parsley and pine nuts for 1–2 minutes. Scatter with the mixed seeds and serve with fish.

ginger

Excellent for the digestive system, ginger heats the body – boosting circulation and metabolism.

Warming ginger is a great spice to add to soups, stews and drinks, helping the body to rid itself of toxins. You can buy ground ginger, but it is far better to look for fresh root ginger that you can grate or chop yourself. Ginger is a natural antiseptic and is rich in the mineral manganese which supports the immune system and is particularly good at fighting off infection, helping to keep you in optimum health while you lose weight.

Ginger is beneficial for nausea, whether caused by morning or motion sickness.

NUTRIENTS
Calcium, magnesium, phosphorus; phenols; volatile oils

GINGER PICKLE

2 tsp fresh lemon juice
2 tsp honey
pinch of salt
2 heaped tsp grated fresh root ginger

This Ayurvedic recipe stimulates and balances the digestive system, extracting maximum nutrition from food. Mix all the ingredients together and take 1 teaspoon 20 minutes before each meal.

index

alfalfa 85
apple 20–21
apricot 22
asparagus 55
aubergine 62
avocado 47
banana 26
barley 78
beetroot 48
Belgian endive *see* chicory 56
berries 30
bio yogurt 110–111
blood sugar 12
broccoli 52–3
brown rice 75
bulgur wheat 70
cabbage 60
calories 12–13
carbohydrates 8–9, 12
carob 121
carrot 37
celeriac 42
celery 66–7
cherry 29
chicken 98
chickpea 82
chicory 56
chilli 124–25
cod 93
courgette 50
cucumber 49
detoxifying 13
duck 104

egg 105
fats 9, 10, 11
fennel 68
fig 19
fromage frais 109
garlic 40
GI (Glycaemic Index) 12
ginger 127
GL (Glycaemic Load) 12
globe artichoke 54
grape 17
grapefruit 35
green tea 113
herbal tea 114
herbs 126
honey 120
intolerances, food 13
juices 116–17
kale 61
kilojoules 13
kiwi fruit 16
leek 41
lemon 33
lentil 80–81
lettuce 63
lime 34
liver 100
low-fat cheese 107
low-fat milk 112
mackerel 91
mango 25
melon 23
mushroom 51
nettle 64

nuts 86
oats 72–3
olives and olive oil 119
onion 38
orange 32
oyster 96
papaya 27
partridge 101
peach 18
pear 24
pine nuts 87
pineapple 15
potato 39
prawn 97
prune 28
psyllium 76
quinoa 77
radish 43
red pepper 46
ricotta cheese 108
rye 71
salmon 90
salt 10
sardine 92
seaweed 69
seeds 88–9
smoothies 118
sorrel 65
soya 83
spices 123
spinach 57
sprouted seeds 84
sugar 10
sweet potato 36

tofu 106
tomato 44–5
tuna 94–5
turkey 99
vegetable bouillon 122
venison 102–103
water 115
watercress 58–9
watermelon 14
wholewheat pasta 79
wild rice 74